A CALL FROM GOD FOR CHANGE

Revelation Received While Resting In The Presence Of The Lord

Zelma McKinney
Minister of God's Word

A Call From God For Change. Revelation Received While Resting in the Presence of the LORD by Zelma McKinney, Minister of God's Word, Dissect My Soul Ministries

www.DissectMySoul.com

Copyright © 2025 Zelma T. McKinney, Dissect My Soul Ministries

All rights reserved. This book or parts thereof may not be reproduced in any form, stored in any retrieval system, or transmitted in any form by any means—electronic, mechanical, photocopy, recording, or otherwise—without prior written permission of the author, except as provided by United States of America copyright law. For permission requests, write to the author at "Attention: Permissions Coordinator" at the address below.

Dissect My Soul Ministries

25060 Hancock Ave., Suite 103-284

Murrieta, CA 92562

holyghostfollowers@dissectmysoul.com

Graphic Design: Melinda Brown

ISBN: 978-1-949509-00-7 E Book

978-1-949509-01-4 Paperback

978-1-949509-02-1 HardCover

Some King James Version (KJV) scripture quotations are from BibleGateway.

www.BibleGateway.com

© 1995-2017, The Zondervan Corporation. All Rights Reserved. The Holy Bible, King James Version. Cambridge Edition: 1769;
King James Bible Online, 2025. www.kingjamesbibleonline.org.© 1995-2017, The Zondervan Corporation. All Rights Reserved.

Scripture quotations taken from the (NASB®) New American Standard Bible®, Copyright © 1960, 1971, 1977, 1995, 2020 by The Lockman Foundation. Used by permission. All rights reserved. lockman.org

Scripture quotations are taken from the Amplified® Bible (AMP), Copyright © 2015 by The Lockman Foundation. Used by permission. lockman.org

Scripture quotations are from the ESV® Bible (The Holy Bible, English Standard Version®), © 2001 by Crossway, a publishing ministry of Good News Publishers. Used by permission. All rights reserved. The ESV text may not be quoted in any publication made available to the public by a Creative Commons license. The ESV may not be translated in whole or in part into any other language.

Scripture quotations marked (NIV) are taken from the Holy Bible, New International Version®, NIV®. Copyright © 1973, 1978, 1984, 2011 by Biblica, Inc.™ Used by permission of Zondervan. All rights reserved worldwide. www.zondervan.comThe "NIV" and "New International Version" are trademarks registered in the United States Patent and Trademark Office by Biblica, Inc.™

Darby Bible Version at www.BibleGateway.com

Scripture quotations from the COMMON ENGLISH BIBLE. © Copyright 2011 COMMON ENGLISH BIBLE. All rights reserved. Used by permission. (www.CommonEnglishBible.com).

Acknowledgments

Writing this book has been a long journey. Subsequent to understanding what God was asking me to do, I immediately started writing. What I had projected would be months to complete actually became years!

As I consider those who need to be acknowledged, above all, I would like to express my heartfelt gratitude to my daughter, TaiVon. God once advised me that the greatest gift He has ever given me is the life of my daughter, who is my only child! This message was delivered by God when all medical professionals were telling me I would never have a child. This gift allowed me to increase my love and awareness of God while instilling deep within my soul the special love and care that parents must always make available to their children. She has been, and continues to be, a close friend and spiritual confidante. She, too, has had most of the spiritual experiences presented in this book. Her unwavering support, encouragement, and understanding have been a constant source of inspiration throughout the process of writing and publishing this work. TaiVon's patience during the many late nights and her insightful feedback have significantly contributed to the development of this book. Her belief in my abilities and her positive energy have motivated me to persevere through challenges and stay committed to my goals as I continue my journey of obedience to my Father God. My prayer has always been that she will not walk away from me as long as I obey God's teachings, which have never seemed normal by earthly standards. I thank God that this prayer continues to be honored. I am deeply grateful for her presence in my life and for the role she has played in making this achievement possible. This acknowledgment is a small token of my appreciation for her love, support, and the joy she brings into my life. I dedicate this book to TaiVon, with all my love and gratitude.

To my grandkids, Raiyn, Skylar, and Zion, I say thank you! During this writing process, I was diagnosed with Rheumatoid Arthritis, Fibromyalgia, RSV, and COVID-19 four times! Whenever I felt as if my pain was too great to carry on…they were there to remind me that Jesus was helping me and to just keep going.

To my husband, George, I am eternally grateful for his love and patience. After 54 years of marriage, we are yet standing by each other in the midst of every storm the enemy of God has thrown our way. God truly destined this marriage, and I love you with all my heart!

I am eternally grateful to ALL the members of Dissect My Soul Ministries (DMSM) for their patience and support over the years. They are the unspoken or hidden treasures that the LORD granted me throughout this process. To them, I declare my love always!

I would be remiss if I do not give a very special Thank You to Rev. Dr. Cecil L. Murray. I was introduced to Pastor Murray a few years ago by a mutual friend. We were seeking possible ways to assist each other in the Lord. I provided him with a copy of my original testimony as I was only beginning to write this book. After reading my testimony, he said he would voluntarily become my disciple, as God had cleared me in his heart. I cried as it was during a period when I was being greatly persecuted. He was very kind in every conversation that we shared. At the time, I did not realize he was a well-known Christian Leader in the Los Angeles area. To me, he was someone who believed in the calling placed upon me by God and encouraged me to go forward. I remember him saying that he would go and do whatever I needed him to as my personal disciple. I found out recently that he passed away, and I will never forget his gentle, kind spirit expressed to an unknown like me. He demonstrated true Christianity! I pray that he is now with the

LORD.

To all those who encouraged me along the way and advised me to never abandon my beliefs or walk away from the perfect will of God …. Thank you very much.

CONTENTS

Acknowledgments i
Foreword 1
Preface 4

Section I

Introduction 10
The Testimony 13
    Pastor's Anniversary Message 23
    Spiritual Realm Revealed 30
    The Reason For My Tears 34
    Understanding The Charge Of God 36
    Who Is Minister Zelma Mckinney? 45
    Testimony Conclusion 52

Section II

Untold Divine Revelations 56
    3/4 Of The Christian World Is On The Way To Hell 59
    The Beginning Before The Beginning 89
    The Sea Is The Assigned Home Of Lucifer/Satan/Demons ... 103
    Woman Is Hated By Satan 115
    The Holy Ghost Is The Female Counterpart Of The Lord ... 119
    Stop Blaming Eve 132
    God's Order Of The Family 136
        Satan's Re-Ordering Of The Family (Phase 1) 137
        Satan's Re-Ordering Of The Family (Phase 2) 138
        Satan's Re-Ordering Of The Family (Phase 3) 139
    Suicide Is Encouraged & Assisted By Satan 146
    Helpless In The Hands Of God 153

Section III

Living A Life Of Job 157
Trust & Obey 167
Testimony After Entering The Presence Of The Lord.............................178
Understanding The Spiritual World..185
Prayer Is The Answer..205
Stir Up The Spirit Of God 214
Evil Has No Face 224
Modern-Day Pharisees 230
"There Is More To This Thing Called Love" Thus Saith The Lord God Almighty . 234

Section IV

What Does It All Mean? 244
Born Again…What Does It Mean? 252
Reading Resources Approved By God...256
Love Is The Answer..266

Section V

Student Testimony #1...272
Student Testimony #2...277
Student Testimony #3...281
Student Testimony #4...284
Student Testimony #5...286

Foreword

How do I begin to talk about a woman of God whom I've personally witnessed walk with Jesus, battle the enemy, and produce spiritual fruit extending into the lives of many others? It may be best to first start with how she touched my life. When we met, I was a foolish young college student who hadn't come to grips with the fact that his Christianity was only surface-deep. One night, I received a call from Zelma, which was most unusual because we didn't talk often. She began and quickly arrived at her point, telling me that Almighty God had given her a message to deliver to me: I was on my way to hell the way I was living. After I hung up, I broke down in tears of remorse and agony. I felt the Lord's piercing rebuke as her words so directly caused me to come face to face with a challenge God had already started putting before my heart. Would I follow Jesus and serve Him, or follow the ways of the world and serve Satan? It was that blunt. I hadn't fully considered my life to be in service of Satan. I knew I struggled unsuccessfully to avoid sin in my life, but I tried to be a good person, or so I thought.

In that phone conversation, God pulled the cover off the

condition of my heart and used Zelma to rebuke me for secret sins that only the Holy Ghost could have revealed. From that night forward, I chose to pursue and follow God Almighty: Father, Son, and Holy Ghost. But at first, I had no idea how to grow in a relationship with the Holy Triune God, what steps to take, or what living a spirit-filled life meant. The Lord again used Zelma for my benefit, as He would have me spend some time visiting with her, hearing her witness about His appearances in her life, and learning about His love for me as evidenced in His holy scriptures. As she shared her testimony and subsequent walk with the Lord, she inspired my own desire to know God in a way that He'd be more real to me than anything else.

Through my many subsequent years of knowing and growing close to her, I've witnessed firsthand her bold faith and steadfast ministry. God has used her to save my sister from the arms of the enemy, deliver my mother from demonic possession, shelter the homeless, comfort the abused, and teach young and old about loving God with all their heart, soul, and strength. She has obeyed God in delivering prophetic messages and revelations, saying what God says to say when He says to say it, and even often delivering uncomfortable messages to unwelcoming audiences. Rejection has not caused her to recoil; slander and persecution have not silenced her, nor have the darts of the devil dissuaded her from speaking the words of the Lord.

Every lesson she teaches is born out of God's personal revelations, which have been given to her but can be validated by God Himself through His Word. Her life is marked by simple principles: Know God and love Him as much as humanly possible, constantly commune with the Holy Ghost for daily guidance and spiritual discernment, and faithfully follow God's instructions no matter how uncomfortable or challenging that may seem. I believe that anyone who reads this book with a heart set on following God's perfect will, will walk away convicted of similar purposes, no matter what state they may enter in. May your life be blessed, as mine has been, by the testimony and ministry of one who sincerely loves Jesus Christ with all her heart.

Sincerely,

Rudy Brown

Preface

This book was written at the charge and command of the LORD God Almighty. God has given me a series of messages on various subjects that will assist humankind in loving Him the way he requires. He asked that I initially present specific warnings to the Christian world but ultimately required that the messages be given to all those who will listen. He explained that although these warnings are intended explicitly for the Christian world, they can be utilized by anyone who wants to learn more about Him. God has watched us go astray for years, witnessing the error of our ways and our lack of understanding of who He is. Therefore, the necessary changes to comply with His desire for the world to love Him truly are presented.

You will find many scripture references throughout this writing. This is by design and as God requested. Rather than debating the meaning of scripture, I was instructed to incorporate it into the body of the messages, making readers accountable for their content. You will often see that I ask you to go to God in prayer with what is presented. What I have to say personally does not compare to what is clearly stated within the scriptures.

Therefore, I ask that you pray as you go.

This book has been divided into sections based on the topical relevancy of the information included. This is specifically for ease in reading and understanding the details intended to benefit the reader and clarify the messages received from the LORD whom I know as "I AM."

For those who are willing to listen with open minds and hearts, we should all arrive at a single truth…absolute truth! I do realize that many do not believe in the concept of absolute truth. While some have even lost their lives for embracing such a belief, I personally do not just believe in this concept; I know it is so due to my knowledge and experience with "I AM." God is Truth. To know God is to understand and walk in the reality of His excellency, recognizing good and evil. From the beginning of time, God never wanted mankind to live outside of His Presence or His Wisdom. However, He also knew that evil would tamper with His Created Man. This was the ultimate plan.

The LORD's initial message charged me to inform the Christian world that His heart is broken due to the actions of the Christian world and that He is not going to wait much longer. God advised that evil is now among us, and we are not equipped to recognize it! He explained that ¾ of the Christian world is on the way to hell and doesn't know it. You will see that this is supported by scripture, as stated in several places identified within this writing.

Many are asking why there is so much chaos occurring in the world today, and where it's coming from? Why is our world environmentally threatened as it is now? What happened to allow such devastation to exist among us? According to God, it all comes from the evil hearts of mankind that are masquerading as good. Such hearts are under the will of the enemy of God, even while He warned us that the devil is a liar and no truth is within him!

> *A good man out of the good treasure of his heart bringeth forth that which is good; and an evil man out of the evil treasure of his heart bringeth forth that which is evil: for of the abundance of the heart his mouth speaketh.*
> *~ Luke 6:45*

This evil is now walking among us and claiming the minds and hearts of all who do not truly love the LORD! This will become clear when you recognize who this enemy is and how the world has been so deceived.

Wars are raging around the world, and America is close to

embracing a Civil War. All of these occurrences are orchestrating as Christianity or in the name of God when they are far from the works and actions of the Living God! God views all these actions as chaos and rooted in evil.

Included within Section I are the details of my personal testimony outlining the path provided by God for me to fall in love with Him. Understanding who I am will help you evaluate the authenticity of my words if the truth is what you seek! God wants my path to be clear to all. Not necessarily to follow it but to understand it. Almost daily, I relive some portion of this journey, which helps keep me focused on His messages and the reality of who He is!

God warned me that although He was sending me to the Christian world with His messages and divine revelations, I would most often be ridiculed, rejected, humiliated, and mocked. Even those who would immediately believe the messages would not be able to hold fast to what they claimed to know and believe. Having received my messages while Resting in the presence of God, this was hard for me to conceive. I know there will be those who will claim that I believe that I am superior to others and have all the answers. I assure you that I do not. Every warning that God is giving and every change that is requested applies to me also. As I receive His messages, I, too, pray for repentance and guidance. Amen.

I sincerely pray that you, as a reader, will go to God in prayer to evaluate the truths of this book. Please allow God to lead you as you go. The enemy of the Lord would love nothing better than for you to rely on your own intellect to determine if my words are true.

Section 2 concentrates on the exact revelations received from God. Many of the chapters in Section 2 are purposely condensed as they may be produced later as stand-alone books to include additional details given by God. There is so much I wish to share with you, and I pray my writings can open your mind and provide an understanding of the spiritual world in which we were created to live. With this understanding, we can all embrace the reality of that which we claim to believe or know. Please pay close attention to this section, which provides divine revelations never before given by God! As difficult as it is to receive these messages at first glance, it does not change the fact that they are true.

Sections 3 and 4 provide theological teachings and navigations of the spiritual world. We can ALL fall in love with Jesus Christ by entering and RESTING in the Presence of the LORD!

Section I

There is no easy way to naturally tell this story so that all can hear and understand, as the Lord has said that there will be those who will arbitrarily reject my statements. The LORD God is Truth and is incapable of lying in any way. It is one thing to say we know God and clearly, another to know that we know the LORD. Throughout this section, I will provide details of my relationship with God and how it came to be. I only ask that you read the entire book before drawing conclusions. In the end, I invite you to question me extensively as you seek the Kingdom of God for the absolute truth of my statements. Amen.

~ 1 ~

Introduction

One day, many years ago, I stood in the presence of the LORD God Almighty. My body, as I knew it, literally stood in His presence. I now know this was a spiritual experience that removed all knowledge of any other form of existence other than what was present. This was not a dream or a vision. What you are about to read might sound untrue or completely unbelievable. I pray that you will seek the LORD for clarification and understanding. He has assured me that anyone who asks will receive confirmation of the absolute truths outlined herein. You are about to take a journey with me and vicariously experience the spiritual teachings and divine revelations I received directly from the mouth of God. I was also told to record many of the spiritual incidents in my life so that others might come to know Him better. He has charged me to go first to the Christian world but ultimately to tell "anyone who has an ear to hear" what He expects from us. He has also charged me with taking you, the reader, down the same growth path that He took me. I know that the LORD works with us in different ways, and I am by no means saying that my story reveals the only pathway to God. I am sure of what I have lived and learned and all God has asked me to reveal. Therefore, the lessons and teachings in this book are those I personally received from the LORD.

Although I believed myself to be a Christian even before my "encounter" with God, I discovered that I was not in the eyes of the LORD God! He was not pleased with who I was. I will explain to you how He was able to change my heart and "save" my life. I will address the path for gaining spiritual wisdom and, more importantly, the tools for "falling in love" with Jesus. **All He wanted was my heart.** He taught me how to love Him by *His* standards. Loving Him as He desires now provides me with a direct corridor for worshiping and resting in His presence whenever I choose to and for as long as I choose to! In His Presence, I get to smell the sweet savor of His Breath, lay my head on His shoulder, and shut out all pain, grief, and cares of the world. When my enemies come against me, I quickly go to Him with a humbled, repentant heart so He can hold me close. Sometimes, I only need to close my eyes, and suddenly, I am in His presence, and nothing else matters. I do not ever need to fight to survive. I simply wrap myself in His arms, and all is well with my soul!

My current work for the LORD stems from the continued work of "Dissect My Soul Ministries," established by the LORD. This teaching ministry shows others how to develop and maintain a "radical" love relationship with God based on what the LORD taught me and instructed me to share with others.

~ 2 ~

The Testimony

It all began in 1986 at a 3-Day Family Reunion in Washington, DC. My family gathered for a Welcome Backyard Barbeque planned as a Hawaiian Luau. As the activities began and I sat by the pool, I suddenly felt very, very heavy. My body felt as though it had been tasked with carrying a ton of bricks. I could not seem to escape this sensation. This weight became heavier and heavier as the night carried on. I felt a mysterious presence with me but could not identify who or what it was. Suddenly, I began to cry. I could not explain the cause of my tears. These were not just small tears but free-flowing tears that consisted of uncontrollable sobbing and moaning. I moved toward the back of the lawn near a gazebo to escape the crowd's attention. Still, family members became concerned and wanted to know what was wrong. No matter how I tried, I could not explain myself to them. "Pull yourself together!" "You are embarrassing us!" were some of the admonitions I received. To save face, I tried to come up with an explanation regarding my father, who had passed away a few years earlier. I was the President of our family reunion and typically the one to keep everything organized and on schedule. Therefore, it was uncharacteristic of me to be isolated from the group while crying for no apparent reason. I spent the remainder of the weekend in a similar state, trying my best to "fit in" and enjoy the weekend, yet feeling utterly broken and saddened.

When I returned home, I found myself still in tears. When I went to work each day, I was in tears. Driving down the street in my car, I was in tears. Wherever I went, I cried. When people in my office began to express concern for me, I would go to the bathroom to cry, so I could not be seen. As it happened, my co-workers noticed me in the bathroom in great despair, so I started using a bathroom on a different floor of the building so that I could cry without anyone knowing who I was. This became my daily life. The tears continued to flow while I was at home as well. My husband tried to help me, but did not know what to do. I could not explain because I genuinely had no known reason for my tears.

After months of crying, I began to pray, "LORD, change me." That is the only thing I could pray for. Everything in my life seemed to be falling apart. My finances were strained, my health had begun to deteriorate, and my friends thought I was having a mental breakdown and began to keep their distance. Even so, I continued to pray, "LORD, change me." About five months later, my 3-year-old daughter was diagnosed with a life-threatening disease, and I could still only bring myself to pray, "LORD, change me." As time passed, my prayer changed to, "LORD, dissect my soul." Not understanding what this meant, I continued to pray this prayer. It was as if I had no choice of what and when to pray. The LORD would only give me these simple words to pray. If I tried to pray using other words, only these words would come forth.

Soon after, I was hospitalized with what appeared to be a heart condition. "Oh, LORD, my God, dissect my soul," I prayed. For months, I had been unable to go to work, attend church, or even leave my home due to my medical condition. While the doctors could find no evidence of an exact heart condition, they treated it as such until they could diagnose what was happening. All at once, I was isolated in what appeared to be the greatest hellhole on earth. I did not recognize my life. The things happening to me physically and emotionally continued to be a mystery that I did not understand, nor could I share with anyone. At some point, the crying became different. It seemed to be coming from a different source within my being. It was more than just tears and sadness now. It had become a desperate, helpless, painful pleading, yet I still did not understand it.

After several months, my existence seemed to be wrapped up in two worlds. I had my life at home with my child and my husband, and I had another life in the spirit, where I was in the presence of God. While in His presence, I found myself in a church, walking back and forth, delivering a speech given to me on a scroll by the LORD. God the Father, Jesus Christ, and the Holy Ghost would sit on the pews. They would tutor, teach, and guide me through every word on the scroll. At the end of our time together, I would be instructed to eat the scroll. I never knew beforehand what was written on the scroll and could never retain its contents afterward. This encounter occurred all the time, during every moment of my day, precisely the same way each time, and I could never escape it. For example, if my body was at home watching TV with my family, instead of my eyes seeing whatever program was broadcasting, I saw myself in the church being tutored by the LORD. While my family slept at night, I found myself in the church delivering the message on the scroll. The reality of being in the presence of God while I practiced this "speech" was all-consuming. Every moment, the LORD presented me with new teachings and definitive instructions regarding the speech on the scrolls.

The most essential thing in the world was what God presented to me. I was consumed by my time in the presence of God, literally ingesting the words He gave me. It felt like just the two of us, or more accurately, the four of us, as I remember Jesus and the Holy Ghost were always present. I do not recall having conversations with my mother, my sisters, my brothers, or any of my friends. The only people I communicated with in my natural life were my husband and my daughter. However, I do remember one member of my church family who often called and expressed her love and concern for me. She will never know how much this meant to me.

Soon after, I was able to return to church. I was not entirely healthy, but I knew the LORD wanted me to be there that day. A visiting guest minister was scheduled to preach that morning. As he spoke, I heard familiar words of things I had received from God over the past year! I was so excited! I recognized his words as words the LORD had spoken in ministering to my spirit. I can't say I would have known these exact words beforehand, but I knew I recognized them at this moment, which comforted my spirit. After the service, I quickly found my way to the front of the church to speak with the minister. I tried to engage him in conversation about his message, eager to understand his perspective.

As I talked about the familiarity of his words and what they meant, I suddenly realized from his expression that he had no idea what I was talking about! It was as if I was referring to a message he did not remember giving! As I looked into his eyes, I found I could see his very soul. What I saw was very sad, like I was looking into an utterly empty vessel. His eyes were unexplainably blank and desolate. His spirit was dead! "How is this possible?" I asked God. I just heard him say many things God Himself had taught me. His eyes told me everything that God wanted me to know. My heart was broken. I did not understand how this could be.

Between the morning and afternoon services, I was approached by one of the church leaders who welcomed me back after being away for such a long time. She said God had answered her prayer, as I had been selected to be the Mistress of Ceremonies at the upcoming Pastor's Anniversary. She had prayed that I would return in time and be able to accept the assignment. As soon as she said this to me, the heavens literally opened, and I heard angelic voices saying, "This is it. Hallelujah, Hallelujah!" And immediately, I knew. I knew that this was what the LORD had been preparing me for. "My LORD," I cried. "No, I cannot give that speech at the Pastor's Anniversary. LORD God, I can't say those things on that scroll! I don't even remember what they are in my conscious mind or what it means!" My spirit was in utter confusion. Although I couldn't recall the details, my spirit was aware that whatever was written on the scrolls God had given me would not be well received by the church. I ran outside the church to get fresh air and to plead with God, "Please don't make me do this. How can I do this? I am no one. I know nothing. I am just a regular woman, LORD." My LORD did not respond.

The rest of the afternoon was miserable. I was restless, anxious, and confused. Soon, God quieted my soul and gave me peace that I cannot explain. I knew unquestionably over the past year that God had been pouring a message into my spirit that would come forth during the Pastor's Anniversary event. I now understood that I had been, and was continuing to be, personally instructed at the hand of God Almighty, the Lord Jesus Christ, and the Holy Ghost. Now, the real work would begin. Knowing God would use me to deliver a specific message to my church brought forth new obstacles of fear, doubt, insecurity, and many works of the enemy to dissuade me from being obedient. With this new understanding of what was happening to me and why, God's teaching method became more intense.

The visits from the LORD continued day in and day out until the designated time the message was to be given. Because I was instructed to eat the scroll after every practice session, I realized that I would be at the total mercy of the LORD on how to proceed, what I must say, and what I must do. I did not have the liberty of "practicing" on my own outside of the presence of God. As soon as my mind began to accept the reality of the task before me, something would come along and tell me that I was delusional! I could feel my spirit battling thoughts from Satan telling me I was crazy. I had no reference for this kind of experience, and at the time, I had never heard of anyone else who had a similar experience. I remember one night reading the Bible as my daughter slept in my arms. In my heart, I prayed, asking God to confirm He was the one I was seeing and hearing. At that moment, all the written words disappeared from the page, and the only words left were "He is the One who has told you." I was so grateful that I fell on my knees and thanked God for that confirmation. Immediately, I could hear the enemy say, "Who is going to believe you?" "Oh God," I cried. "How can anyone be expected to live this way?"

Satan's thoughts continued to plague me. Another night, I found myself kneeling in a bedroom alone as I pleaded with God to help me understand, telling Him what Satan was saying seemed genuine! Nobody would ever believe me if I told them about my experience. I vowed to God that if He would show me, without a shadow of a doubt, that He was the one speaking to me, I would never question Him again! I asked that He reveal Himself to me in a way that no man, woman, child, or anything in this universe could ever shake my faith and understanding of who He is.

Not a second later, I found myself on a mountaintop. I was in the presence of the LORD God Almighty and Moses! God was to my right, yet He was everywhere around me! He was greater than anything I have ever seen or could imagine! Wherever I looked, He was there; to the right, left, up, and down, He was there. He was everywhere. Moses was to my left on one bent knee with his head in his hands. I wish I could say it was a beautiful sight, but it was not. God was angry with me. He spoke in a **"terrible"** voice that was all-encompassing yet empowering. He said to me:

> *"How dare you ask me again to explain who I Am! I have revealed myself to you over and*

> *over and over! I AM THAT I AM THAT I AM. When others question your calling, tell them that I AM CALLED YOU. When you teach, let them know that you are representing the words and truths of I AM."*

I was in the presence of God all night long on my knees as I listened to His all-consuming voice. When daybreak arrived, I was still on my knees but was now in my bedroom. I stood up, felt drawn to look at myself in the mirror, and knew I was not the same. **I was changed!** I did not look the same as I had before. My face, literally, looked different. I certainly did not feel the same. My entire being was changed. I had an assurance of having been in the presence of the LORD, hearing His voice, and knowing the truth and reality of my encounter with Him. I walked out of that room without a doubt that I had stood in the very presence of the Great I AM! I purposed in my heart that day I would forever listen to and obey Him. I also knew that going forward, it would not matter if anyone believed me. God had, in fact, revealed Himself to me in a way that no one could ever cause me to doubt Him or the experience of standing in His presence. He had answered my prayer.

… **3** …

Pastor's Anniversary Message

The Pastor's Anniversary arrived. As **God would have it, I gave that message to my church, standing on absolute faith.** I had no idea what I was going to say or when. I was extremely nervous, but I trusted God all the way. As I sat there waiting for the program to start, the LORD took me around the sanctuary to let me see part of the problems in the church as viewed through His eyes. There was internal mumbling coming from the people, which did not come from their mouths but from inside of them as audible voices! I heard the most vulgar, despicable, hateful words spoken. Yet on their faces were painted pretty smiles and expressions that seemed Christian-like. God explained what I heard were the words and attitudes actually in their hearts! *"See how they lie with their mouths, and the heart reveals the truth of who they are."* I was greatly disturbed by what I saw and could feel the pain of the LORD as He looked at those who were supposed to be His people. The audience was packed, and I knew spiritual forces were also all around. Little did I know my life was about to change profoundly. I would soon discover what had happened to me over the past year and why I could not dry the tears from my eyes.

Finally, I was given the OK to start the program. I carefully stood up and began to follow the written program I had been given. I had no idea when or how the message from God would be given. Suddenly, along with everyone in the audience, I heard my mouth say:

> *"I am going to deviate from the program at this point. I have a message for you from the LORD. God appeared to me and gave me a message for this church."*

As these words came from my mouth, I could not believe what I heard. "What am I saying?" I thought. I had no control over my words and could not stop the flow. I noticed I was walking and moving back and forth before the audience, just as I had during my "practice sessions" with the LORD. As I continued to speak, I heard my mouth say:

> *"God appeared to me and flashed my life before my face. He showed me who I was. He*

told me that I was good and that I had been a good person all of my life. He also told me that goodness was not enough and that HE DID NOT KNOW ME. He started to cry as He looked at me, and as tears rolled down His face, He slowly walked away from me. My heart ached with a pain that I cannot describe, and I cried uncontrollably for hours that turned into months and eventually into a year! I had no understanding of why I was crying. I simply knew that something had changed in my life. Something that had been so right in my life was now extremely wrong. Everywhere I went, I cried. I tried to pray but could only cry. The message I am about to give you from God will be validated by our guest speaker tonight. He will repeat exactly what I am about to say."

"Oh, LORD God," my spirit cried. "Now I understand. Come back to me and show me how to live for you alone! Please look into my heart and know that no one means more to me than You do. I am willing to always be helpless in your hands." My soul was at peace at last. He revealed Himself to me and the church. God had a message for all aspects of the church that night. He begged the people to stop sinning and come back to Him. He had a message for the Pastor, Ministerial Staff, Deacons, Ushers, the Choir, and the congregation. No one was left out.

As God continued to speak through me that night, He informed the church the guest preacher who would deliver the evening's message would confirm my words to the church in 5 points. This was foretold so the audience could tangibly validate the message I delivered. As the speaker stood, he opened up his pre-written message. Shockingly, he found every item God spoke about on his paper! He tried his best to avoid saying what God had previously revealed he would say. I could see him struggling, hesitating, pausing, and doing everything he could to say something other than the things I had stated he would say. Unbelievably, to all present, he did not even start with #1 of his 5 points. This was apparent as he called out the number of each item as he spoke, which made it clear that he had skipped the previous numbers listed on his page. He continued to move erratically, seeking a way to avoid validating the message given to the church. By the time he was finished, he had, in fact, given all 5 points previously spoken by the LORD God! The church was speechless, as was I.

God had warned me that only a handful of people would believe what they had heard that night. He also said that soon afterward, they, too, would forget. True to His word, about five people approached me after the program and wanted to hear more about how God had appeared to me. We went to one of the Deacons' homes to pray.

After completing God's assignment that night, I went home and slept like a newborn baby. I was so at peace. A few nights later, it started all over again. Once again, I was daily in the presence of the LORD. I did not understand. I had given the message, and I thought that God was pleased. God informed me that the original message might have been for my church, but it was actually intended for the whole world, specifically the Christian world. He then charged me to deliver His messages to all who were willing to listen. Here are the Words of the LORD God:

> *"Say to the Christian world that my heart is broken at the state of the Christian world. ¾ of the Christian world is on its way to hell, and don't know it. They are practicing Christianity in their own way, and they never asked me what it means to be a Christian. Tell them that I am not going to wait much longer."*

God taught me never to fear what I would speak or teach on His behalf. He said that every word I would preach or teach had already been placed in my belly, as I had literally "eaten" His words on the scrolls He had given me. He said to me, "Stand, and I will speak." The spiritual transformation continued. God let me know that there was so much more that I had to be taught. During this time, He spoon-fed me extraordinary wisdom and divine revelations. He taught me how to love others as He loved them. He walked me through the scriptures of the Holy Bible and provided Divine understanding.

Subsequently, God called me to preach and teach. This was a challenging period for me, as my Pastor was still very resentful of the message spoken to the church. He refused to acknowledge my call from God to preach. Our small Illinois church had just completed the construction of a multi-million-dollar facility. They would repeatedly schedule the opening date, only to have it canceled each time. God had told me that until the Pastor accepted my calling and allowed me to become a part of the Ministerial Staff, they would NEVER move into the new facility! Finally, one Saturday night, I received a call from the Assistant Pastor informing me I was invited to join the Ministerial Staff the following day. Within one week after that day, we moved into the new facility by the Grace of God!

My fellow church members tried to convince me to get over

my "little encounter" with God. They said it meant nothing, and I should move on with my life. I could not receive this advice, as I then knew the reality of the LORD God Almighty. My understanding of the dire state of the Christian world was beginning to take shape.

~ 4 ~

Spiritual Realm Revealed

I was forever at peace in the presence of the LORD. I enjoyed just sitting at His feet and hanging on to His every word. I thought this would forever be my role. As my health recovered, God prevented me from returning to my job, which I had loved tremendously. Instead, He had me open a custom clothing store. I could not sew! Yet, He taught me how to sew. I will explain more about this subject later in this essay. However, it was in this arena that God started to introduce me to the spiritual realm. I learned about the mystery surrounding the requirement for Levitical Priests to wear specific fabrics. God exposed many of the tactics used by Satan and the demonic world, specifically against Christians. I saw and heard things no "natural" mind or eye is capable of understanding or seeing.

The instructions on the angelic and holy realm were, and continue to be, amazing in all ways. The dark side of the spiritual realm was initially extremely frightening. I asked God why He was showing me these things and why it was necessary for me to know. He then reminded me of something I had once said to Him. I told God I wanted to know EVERYTHING about Him. I told him that I was a perfectionist in everything I do, and I didn't want someone else to know him in a way I didn't. If He was going to be my Father, I expected Him to share with me as a Father would. I had no idea what I was saying! As I later studied the scriptures, I was surprised to discover that even Moses had requested the same thing from God! He wanted to experience ALL of God and fully understand and see His Glory. Moses' request is found in the scripture below:

> *Now therefore, I pray thee, if I have found grace in thy sight, shew me now thy way, that I may know thee, that I may find grace in thy sight: and consider that this nation is thy people. ~ Exodus 33:13*

God explained to me that for Him to grant my prayer to know all of Him, I needed to know His enemy as intimately as I knew Him. He let me know there was no reason to fear, and HE would NEVER leave me alone! God has honored this promise, even to this day!

He gave me the gift of Discernment of Spirits, allowing me

to see, know, and understand the inner workings of the spiritual realm. Through this gift, He guides me into a deeper spiritual understanding of the distinction between "true vs. false" Christianity. I had, and continue to have, many visitations by unclean and demonic spirits trying to stunt my growth in Christ or stop the work with which I have been charged. I have also experienced the visitations of angelic helpers from the LORD. The deaths of my family members and my own death have been aborted many times at the will of God with His angelic beings.

    I had to learn how to live with the gift of Discernment of Spirits. You see, it is not only about seeing invisible demonic spirits; it is also about seeing the true human spirit of mankind. At the beginning of trying to manage this gift, I would speak with a person and see more than one mouth talking and multiple sets of eyes looking back at me. The numerous words that proceeded from their mouth had different meanings. God was able to show me that this was precisely what he had allowed me to witness on the night of the original message to my church. It wasn't very comforting to see multiple eyes housed within their original eyes. All of these eyes were looking in different directions. I could smell awful odors coming from both the invisible and visible beings. I used to run and hide in my house, pleading with God to take it away. He refused to alter His instructions. He continued to teach and refine my understanding. Imagine, for a moment, standing before someone and hearing them express words of encouragement or preach or speak truths in Christ Jesus, and then see the evil spirits inside as clearly as you see them physically. How would you respond to this? God had to teach me how to handle it. God explained that this is why He does not listen to the words of our mouths but discerns our obedience and love for Him based on the contents of our hearts. Many pretend to worship Him, but their heart is far from Him. I am incredibly grateful that God alone knows my thoughts and how much I love Him. He has taught me how to always remain in His presence. For this, too, I am grateful.

~ 5 ~

The Reason for My Tears

Through the original message to my church, I understood the reason for my tears that had lasted almost a year. I had been crying because God had appeared before me and allowed my human spirit to commune with His Holy Spirit. Then He walked away. Being in His presence allowed my human spirit to come "alive" and recognize His Spirit. At that moment, my human spirit was born again or regenerated, and I knew Him as God. As He walked away, He became less evident to my human spirit. As He withdrew from before me, my human spirit began to grieve and moan for His presence. I tried searching for him, but He was nowhere to be found. I began to panic and plead for Him to return and teach me what I must do to remain in His presence. I begged Him to show me how to be better than good. That was the essence of my prayers: "LORD, change me" and "LORD, dissect my soul." I so desperately needed Him to come back to me. His absence was such a devastating blow to my human spirit. It forced me to search fervently to regain whatever it was that I had discovered. As time passed and He was completely removed from the "sight" of my human spirit, my spirit became "dead" again. I was no longer "alive" and able to be in His presence. I knew I would never again be content outside the presence of the LORD! Even though I had no idea what was missing from my life at the time or why I was crying in my conscious state, my human spirit did know. It was created to live in the presence of God and is only functional and complete when empowered by the Holy Ghost Spirit of God. Because I gave my all to seek the truth of what was happening to me, God "dissected my soul" and regenerated my spirit. As a Master Surgeon, He removed everything about and within me that was not pleasing in His sight. When He revealed Himself to me again, He taught me what it truly means to be a Christian. I would never function again outside of this new experience. I later became aware of the truth and power of what Jesus was saying to Nicodemus in the following scripture: "…Verily, verily, I say unto thee, except a man be born again, he cannot see the kingdom of God." ~ *John 3:3*. That had truly been my experience. My spirit saw Him and knew Him as I stood in His presence. As soon as He vanished, my human spirit died, and I could no longer "see the kingdom of God!"

~ 6 ~

Understanding the Charge of God

For over 30 years, I have honored God's charge to me. I accepted this spiritual assignment of taking the message of God to the Christian world, believing that I had an easy task. I was initially grateful that God was sending me to the Christian world. I thought I was being sent among "friends" and true believers. As God looked at me with His all-knowing eyes, He knew and understood how innocent and naïve I was to think such a thing. When given this charge, I once again saw tears in His eyes. I remember saying, "God, I will tell them. I will make them understand. When they hear my story, they will believe and know that you truly are God!" He walked away as I heard Him say in my spirit, "My child, you will soon see and understand."

There is so much more to my testimony of living in the presence of the great "I AM." To many, my words are unbelievable and will not be received. Despite my testimony and love for God, I have been, and continue to be, greatly persecuted, mainly by the Christian world. This makes the scripture below very personal to me. I know I will always prevail over the spirits of darkness and the intentional evil acts of mankind. No one can take away my testimony or cause me to doubt the great "I AM." I hold on to the scripture below for added comfort:

> *"And they overcame him by the blood of the Lamb and by the word of their testimony; and they loved not their lives unto the death."*
> *~ Revelation 12:11*

I have presented only a tiny portion of my testimony and walk with God in this section. More specific details will be provided within the proper context throughout this writing. Just understand that I received from the LORD all that I know. The primary key my Father God has given me is the power of prayer. It is through prayer that He taught me to enter into His presence. God desires all souls to connect with His Holy Spirit and learn of and commune with Him. The LORD God seeks those who will always love Him… at all costs. When we surrender our hearts to the Lord Jesus Christ, he "saves" us from the darkness of this world by placing us in a bubble of protection as we grow spiritually. When we are no longer "babes in Christ," Jesus presents us to God the Father. It is at this point that the Holy

Ghost takes charge of our souls to guide us through all understanding and safekeeping. We begin to understand that we should come to Him in prayer, not asking or seeking anything other than His Holy Presence. It is time for Christian leaders to recognize the importance of teaching others how to "fall in love" with Jesus Christ. As we demonstrate our love for Christ, He investigates our hearts and accepts our worship of Him as God. Pray for a true understanding of the scripture below:

Romans 10:1-11

¹ Brethren, my heart's desire and prayer to God for Israel is that they might be saved.
² For I bear them record that they have a zeal of God, but not according to knowledge.
³ For they being ignorant of God's righteousness, and going about to establish their own righteousness, have not submitted themselves unto the righteousness of God.
⁴ For Christ is the end of the law for righteousness to every one that believeth.
⁵ For Moses describeth the righteousness which is of the law, That the man which doeth those things shall live by them.
⁶ But the righteousness which is of faith speaketh on this wise, Say not in thine heart,

Who shall ascend into heaven? (that is, to bring Christ down from above:)
⁷ Or, Who shall descend into the deep? (that is, to bring up Christ again from the dead.)
⁸ But what saith it? The word is nigh thee, even in thy mouth, and in thy heart: that is, the word of faith, which we preach;
⁹ That if thou shalt confess with thy mouth the LORD Jesus, and shalt believe in thine heart that God hath raised him from the dead, thou shalt be saved.
¹⁰ For with the heart man believeth unto righteousness, and with the mouth, confession is made unto salvation.
¹¹ For the scripture saith, Whosoever believeth on him shall not be ashamed.

In the preceding scripture, Paul warns the people of the need to become acquainted with the actual "righteousness" of God. He explains that they had a "zeal" for wanting to know God, but had no idea who God really is. This scripture clearly demonstrates that Israel had developed its own way of knowing God rather than doing it God's way! Paul made it clear to them that God does not listen to what we say with our mouths but rather to what He sees in our hearts. Unfortunately, many would-be believers are being misled, even today, to believe they are "saved" because of what they are saying with their mouths! While no man can judge the salvation of another, it is also true that out of context, this notion perpetuates the same act of "going about to establish their own righteousness" that Paul refers to in the above scriptures. God will hold EVERYONE involved in this practice accountable for leading His Souls down this road of destruction!

False religion is a significant stronghold Satan uses in today's church. Everyone wants to believe that their agenda is the right one. All God wants is for us to make His agenda number one in our hearts. Is it so difficult to have no doctrinal views at all? The only doctrine we need is captured in Romans 10:9-11. He only asks that we love Him with all our heart, mind, and soul! He also commands that we love one another. We need to love Him with a **"radical, fervent"** love that transforms us into what He desires for us. Loving God in this manner has allowed me to rest daily in His presence. There is no other place I would rather be.

God changed me. **He dissected my soul.** A comprehensive guide to this process will be provided in later chapters. The present explanation is in order for me to be used by God, He had to make me helpless in all areas of my life. No one was allowed to "help" me during my period of change. God made me rely totally on him. As His Messenger, I needed to be absolutely connected to His Spirit. He taught me what it means to be **"born again"** and live for Him and in Him.

Because God told me that the message I delivered that night to my church was to be delivered to the Christian world, my eyes are continuously opened to see the church's lack of understanding of the reality of who God is. For those who might not believe that He instructed me to tell the Christian world that three-fourths of the Christian world is on its way to hell and don't know it, consider the scripture below to validate God's message:

Mark 4:3-9

³ Hearken; Behold, there went out a sower to sow:
⁴ And it came to pass, as he sowed, some fell by the way side, and the fowls of the air came and devoured it up.
⁵ And some fell on stony ground, where it had not much earth; and immediately it sprang up, because it had no depth of earth:
⁶ But when the sun was up, it was scorched; and because it had no root, it withered away.
⁷ And some fell among thorns, and the thorns grew up, and choked it, and it yielded no fruit.
⁸ And other fell on good ground, and did yield fruit that sprang up and increased; and

brought forth, some thirty, and some sixty, and some an hundred.
⁹ And he said unto them, He that hath ears to hear, let him hear.

Jesus explained to his disciples that the mystery of the parable was for them to know and understand. In essence, God withholds the truths of His word from those who have not fully surrendered their hearts to Him. The majority of the crowd listening to this parable did not receive an explanation of its meaning. God judged that many of them fell into the first 3 of the four categories outlined in the parable and, therefore, were not fit to receive His divine revelation. To the one-fourth, God gave them ears to hear what the Spirit of God was saying. See His clarification in the scriptures below:

Mark 4:10-20

¹⁰ And when he was alone, they that were about him with the twelve asked of him the parable.
¹¹ And he said unto them, Unto you it is given to know the mystery of the kingdom of God: but unto them that are without, all these things are done in parables:
¹² That seeing they may see, and not perceive; and hearing they may hear, and not understand; lest at any time they should be

converted, and their sins should be forgiven them.

¹³ And he said unto them, Know ye not this parable? and how then will ye know all parables?

¹⁴ The sower soweth the word.

¹⁵ And these are they by the way side, where the word is sown; but when they have heard, Satan cometh immediately, and taketh away the word that was sown in their hearts.

¹⁶ And these are they likewise which are sown on stony ground; who, when they have heard the word, immediately receive it with gladness;

¹⁷ And have no root in themselves, and so endure but for a time: afterward, when affliction or persecution ariseth for the word's sake, immediately they are offended.

¹⁸ And these are they which are sown among thorns; such as hear the word,

¹⁹ And the cares of this world, and the deceitfulness of riches, and the lusts of other things entering in, choke the word, and it becometh unfruitful.

²⁰ And these are they which are sown on good ground; such as hear the word, and receive it, and bring forth fruit, some thirtyfold, some sixty, and some an hundred.

As you can see from the scriptures above, there are four categories in the parable Jesus Christ gave to His disciples. Those who fall in either of the top three categories that are outside the will of God are following Satan and are lost. They are the ¾ that are on the way to hell and don't know it!

~ 7 ~

Who Is Minister Zelma McKinney?

God has given me three offices in which to operate. He has called me as a Minister, Teacher, and Messenger. As a Minister and Teacher, I am afforded greater latitude in my tolerance of others and their perspectives on the Gospel of Jesus Christ. However, such tolerance does not change what God has ordained me to teach. I must teach and minister that which He has given me. This cannot be abandoned! My teachings are not as the world understands but as He has spoken to me. This does not mean I know everything, but I KNOW what He has said! I always seek opportunities to learn and grow, and God is still teaching me. I take everything I hear from others back to God for clarification and understanding. I know enough about God to understand that we never reach a point where we can rely solely on our own experience of anything. We must always be prepared to take everything to God in prayer.

As a Messenger of the LORD, I have no control over what I speak. I speak what my Father instructs at the time He instructs!

This often leads others to misunderstand me or to question my motives. I am frequently accused of rebelling against authority for speaking God's truths. I pray you can receive my written words and take them back to God for a deeper understanding.

The scrolls God had me eat each night of our private sessions contained every message I will ever give, Thus saith the LORD. I do not know what they are until God opens my mouth to speak. This trusting relationship of being His Messenger, as charged to me by God, bears witness in several places in the Holy Scriptures. Consider the following with the call of Ezekiel:

Ezekiel 3:1-10

> *[1] "Moreover he said unto me, Son of man, eat that thou findest; eat this roll, and go speak unto the house of Israel.*
> *[2] So I opened my mouth, and he caused me to eat that roll.*
> *[3] And he said unto me, Son of man, cause thy belly to eat and fill thy bowels with this roll that I give thee. Then did I eat it; and it was in my mouth as honey for sweetness.*
> *[4] And he said unto me, Son of man, go, get thee unto the house of Israel, and speak with my words unto them.*

> *⁵ For thou art not sent to a people of a strange speech and of an hard language, but to the house of Israel;*
>
> *⁶ Not to many people of a strange speech and of an hard language, whose words thou canst not understand. Surely, had I sent thee to them, they would have hearkened unto thee.*
>
> *⁷ But the house of Israel will not hearken unto thee; for they will not hearken unto me: for all the house of Israel are impudent and hardhearted.*
>
> *⁸ Behold, I have made thy face strong against their faces, and thy forehead strong against their foreheads.*
>
> *⁹ As an adamant harder than flint have I made thy forehead: fear them not, neither be dismayed at their looks, though they be a rebellious house. ¹⁰ Moreover he said unto me, Son of man, all my*
> *words that I shall speak unto thee receive in thine heart, and hear with thine ears."*

Just as God knew Israel would not hearken unto Ezekiel, He quickly revealed that the Christian world would not hearken unto me! I know it is not about whether people listen but rather about my obedience to tell them what He says! Many people disbelieve and try to convince me to change my teachings to conform to a doctrinal view that differs from what God Almighty reveals directly to me. I cannot be moved. I have purposed in my heart before my God Almighty that *I AM NOT COMING OFF THE WALL!* Nehemiah declared in the scripture below that he could not come down because he knew what God had said and instructed him to do. No matter what scheme others devised to change his mind, he remained firm in his statement that he could not come down.

I have witnessed evil-hearted men and women pretending to be living for Christ use many acts of deception in their attempts to get me to abandon my faith and my testimony of Jesus Christ. Consider the steadfastness displayed in the scripture below. I, too, will NEVER leave or walk away from what God has spoken. He has placed a "born again" spirit inside me, which allows me to bask in His presence daily. Because of who He is, I am madly in love with Him! I have learned to involve Him in every thought of mine. It makes all the difference in who I am and what I do.

Nehemiah 6:1-3; 8,10-14 (Darby)

[1] And it came to pass when Sanballat, and Tobijah, and Geshem the Arabian, and the rest of our enemies, heard that I had built the wall and that there was no breach left in it (though at that time I had not set up the doors in the gates),

² that Sanballat and Geshem sent to me, saying, Come, let us meet together in the villages in the plain of Ono. But they thought to do me mischief.

³ And I sent messengers to them, saying, I am doing a great work, and I cannot come down. Why should the work cease, whilst I leave it and come down to you?

⁸ And I sent to him, saying, There are no such things done as thou sayest, but thou feignest them out of thine own heart.

¹⁰ And I came to the house of Shemaiah the son of Delaiah, the son of Mehetabeel, who had shut himself up. And he said, Let us meet together in the house of God, within the temple, and let us shut the doors of the temple; for they are coming to kill thee; even in the night are they coming to kill thee.

¹¹ And I said, Should such a man as I flee? and who is there, that, being as I am, could go into the temple, and live? I will not go in.

¹² And I perceived, and behold, God had not sent him; for he pronounced this prophecy against me; and Tobijah and Sanballat had hired him.

¹³ Therefore was he hired, that I should be afraid, and do so, and sin, and that they might have wherewith to spread an evil report, that they might reproach me.

¹⁴ My God, remember Tobijah and Sanballat according to these their works, and also the prophetess Noadiah, and the rest of the prophets who would have put me in fear.

Biographically, I was born in the south in the small town of Pelham, Georgia, as one of eight children. I was reared by my grandparents, Ella and Mozell Porter, from the age of 3. My grandmother is the only person I know who has truly embodied the principles she found within the Christian Gospels. As such, she taught me to love and respect the scriptures of the Bible. I now understand that this love was crucial in laying the foundation necessary to receive the appearances and teachings of "I AM" as my LORD.

I graduated from Florida A&M University with a bachelor's degree in Speech and Hearing Pathology. I also became certified in reading and Learning Disabilities. After teaching for a few years, I obtained a master's degree in Mental Retardation from Ball State University.

I worked as an educator for 10 years before changing careers. I began a 30+ year career in Insurance Claims adjustment and Quality Control. This allowed me to communicate with judges, attorneys, and insurance carriers around the world. I found that most insurance companies weren't interested in fairness or doing the right thing; instead, they aligned their views with what served their best interests.

I have come to understand that God inspired all my career choices. He used these situations to eliminate pain and stress in the lives of others and to heal the hearts of the forgotten and downtrodden that were being unrightly projected by the hands of evil!

~ 8 ~

Testimony Conclusion

I found Jesus Christ through those months of helplessly seeking His face. I came to know Him as the Great "I AM THAT I AM THAT I AM!" I know the God that revealed Himself to me IS God! Do you believe God is yet speaking to His people? Suppose you are a teacher/minister/preacher or anyone guiding the souls of God's people. Are you teaching them to enter a personal, intimate love relationship with the Lord Jesus Christ? What are you waiting for? Please do it while there is still time. Amen.

My prayer for those reading this book is that they will seek the face of the LORD for clarity and understanding. Please do not judge me or my words based on your own understanding. God has assured me that if anyone seeks Him for answers, He will respond. If you are one of those individuals who believe I have lost my way, then pray for me as I pray for you. God will judge us both.

I am always available to answer questions for anyone

wishing to know more about my encounters with the great I AM THAT I AM. If you know and believe in God, you should have many questions. If you do not have a relationship with the LORD God Almighty, you should have even more questions. You can reach me through my ministry website for more information. (www.dissectmysoul.com).

May you be forever blessed in all you do for the LORD GOD. Amen.

Section II

In Section I, I tried my best to explain how I met the LORD and how I came to love Him with my whole heart. I have shared many things God taught me that made the difference in acquiring a "radical" love relationship with Him rather than being a mediocre believer. To grasp the relevance and urgency of the need for all created souls to become one with "I AM" and to rest in His presence, you must first believe what has already been presented. Should you not believe in the reality that God truly is God, that Jesus Christ, as the Living Son of God, is also Savior of all, you will not comprehend the importance or necessity of Resting in the Presence of the LORD!

Throughout Section II, my discussions will center around the things learned while **Resting in the Presence of the LORD**. The most important section in this writing contains Divine Revelations received directly from the LORD God Almighty. It is through following and understanding these revelations that I have been able to listen, hear, follow, and obey the LORD. Here, I developed a greater love and dependency on the Holy Ghost! I knew that trying to understand the Spiritual Truths of God would never be known based on my own intellect or the teachings from the natural or physical world.

Through God's teachings and revelations, I better understand the scriptures and mysteries referenced in the Bible. No matter what you do, please read these revelations with an open mind. I intend to create each revelation as a stand-alone book as it is too difficult to explain all the aspects in this writing.

~ 9 ~

Untold Divine Revelations

The Bible is filled with untold mysteries proclaimed by those who received them directly from Jesus Christ Himself. God speaks many truths to His followers that can never last or endure within the soul of those not abiding within the righteous realm of "I AM."

I sit here again today with pain deep within my soul! "How do I explain this, my Lord? I ask. The words of your mouth and your teachings are so profound and holy that they become very sacred! I'm watching lies spew from the mouths of bystanders led by the devil. These liars claim to know you. How can that be? Do they not understand that you know even the intent of all their thoughts and actions? Who taught them to search out and follow your righteousness, Lord? How can they see or understand their own betrayal if they don't know you as you desire? The work of your enemy is displayed. The devil is cunning and seeks day-to-day to capture the souls of your people.

My deep pain comes from understanding the mysteries

revealed by God. Like Jonah, I often have considered not telling the Christian world what the Lord is saying! This thought, I know, comes not from God but from the adversary of my Lord. Just as Jonah did not know the actions that Nineveh would take when God's message was delivered, I have no real insight into how others will receive this book. My only responsibility is to repeat the revelations to anyone who has an ear to hear and those who are willing to listen.

The LORD has shown me that the reading of the scriptures alone will not provide the absolute authentic truth of all things righteous and holy. I grew up reading the Bible and believing I was truly living for God. Subsequently, I came to know my life was not pleasing to the Lord! To love God is to KNOW Him. Without knowing God, it is impossible to understand His ways and actions! To love God is the first prerequisite to being known as a "True" Christian. Jesus Himself declared that many would call Him by name and yet not know Him!

> *And why call ye me, Lord, Lord, and do not the things which I say? ~ Luke 6:46*
>
> *A good man out of the good treasure of his heart bringeth forth that which is good; and an evil man out of the evil treasure of his heart*

> *bringeth forth that which is evil: for of the abundance of the heart his mouth speaketh.*
> *~ Luke 6:45*

It is almost impossible to list all things taught to me by God. However, He instructed several mysteries to be told. There is no way for me to prove to you any of the information provided. I am simply required to tell you what He is saying. The mysteries presented here show the need to issue a stark warning to the world to reconsider our ways and actions as self-confessing Christians! I am convinced many prayers will be answered upon reading my words, and deeper instruction will be provided to those who have been seeking additional clarification of the subjects presented.

~ 10 ~

3/4 of the Christian World
Is on the Way to Hell

> [19] *Nevertheless the foundation of God standeth sure, having this seal, The Lord knoweth them that are his. And, Let every one that nameth the name of Christ depart from iniquity.*
> [20] *But in a great house there are not only vessels of gold and of silver, but also of wood and of earth; and some to honour, and some to dishonour.*
> [21] *If a man therefore purge himself from these, he shall be a vessel unto honour, sanctified, and meet for the master's use, and prepared unto every good work.*
> [22] *Flee also youthful lusts: but follow righteousness, faith, charity, peace, with them that call on the Lord out of a pure heart.*
> [23] *But foolish and unlearned questions avoid, knowing that they do gender strifes.*
> [24] *And the servant of the Lord must not strive; but be gentle unto all men, apt to teach, patient,*
> [25] *In meekness instructing those that oppose themselves; if God peradventure will give them repentance to the acknowledging of the truth;*
> [26] *And that they may recover themselves out of the snare of the devil, who are taken captive by him at his will.*
> *~ 2 Timothy 2: 19-26*

My words might not initially appear to be believable, but the scriptures above give us all the opportunity to seek God with assurance that He will respond. The first step is to develop a "Radical" love relationship with God, as described in the 63rd Psalm below. This scripture highlights the depths to which David went to perfect his love relationship with God. It also demonstrates that an abiding nature was achieved, and loving protection provided by God.

Psalm 63:1-11 (NIV)
A psalm of David. When he was in the Desert of Judah.

¹ You, God, are my God, earnestly I seek you; I thirst for you, my whole being longs for you, in a dry and parched land where there is no water.
² I have seen you in the sanctuary and beheld your power and your glory.
³ Because your love is better than life, my lips will glorify you.
⁴ I will praise you as long as I live, and in your name I will lift up my hands.
⁵ I will be fully satisfied as with the richest of foods; with singing lips my mouth will praise you.
⁶ On my bed I remember you; I think of you through the watches of the night.

> ^{7} *Because you are my help, I sing in the shadow of your wings.*
> ^{8} *I cling to you; your right hand upholds me.*
> ^{9} *Those who want to kill me will be destroyed; they will go down to the depths of the earth.*
> ^{10} *They will be given over to the sword and become food for jackals.*
> ^{11} *But the king will rejoice in God; all who swear by God will glory in him, while the mouths of liars will be silenced.*

For years, I have lived with the revelation from the LORD that the Christian world needs truth…His truth! I have made it my life's goal to tell as many people as possible what the LORD is saying. With each telling, my heart breaks as I witness the listeners' lack of understanding or non-belief. I have met with church leaders, Pastors, Evangelists, Ministers, Bible teachers, self-proclaiming Christians, business leaders, and atheists. Overwhelmingly, the response has always been the same. They do not believe that my words are true. Many have even said that God no longer speaks. Oh God, how this breaks my heart! They tell me that everything God wants His people to know is already recorded in the scriptures. This is incredibly sad and shows a lack of understanding of who God is. Do we serve a dead God? Is He a God made of wood or stone, no different from the idol gods referenced in the Bible? God forbid!

The LORD continuously points out to me that the church (those who claim to know Him) does not believe me because they believe He is dead. How awful! Without realizing my own motives, God subsequently showed me that I was out to prove Him wrong rather than accept the Christian denials. The LORD can never be wrong, so what did He mean? I discovered I was so convinced that when self-confessing true believers heard my words and questioned me extensively about the messages from the LORD, they would be convinced and believe. It has been one of the most heartbreaking experiences of my life to witness the church's lack of understanding. The LORD allowed me to see I was correct in my assumption of their potential belief…if they were true believers! As in the 63rd Psalm, the love and protection of our Lord and Savior, Jesus Christ, can satisfy our needs above everything else.

The real problem stems from man's lack of understanding of God Almighty and/or the Holy Ghost. They lack knowledge of the profound impact of the spiritual world upon our lives. Most people do not even believe there is a spiritual world or understand that we are spirits living in a natural world. Everything we do is impacted by the spiritual world, whether we believe it or not. This lack of understanding benefits only the enemy of God.

There must be a proper understanding of who God the Father is before one can claim to have a relationship with Him! Unfortunately, "would-be" believers are being taught they only need to say they are "Christians" when they do not understand what this means. ***The church leaders God charges to present Him to the world have failed***. I struggle profoundly to understand how this is possible since "knowing God" is simple! Before taking the title "Christian," the "soul" must be abandoned to the LORD. The soul then agrees to take on the character of the LORD and follow His teaching. Such a one must be willing to be like Him in every way and, more importantly, to be guided by the Wisdom of the Holy Ghost. I know we can never be perfect, as the LORD is, but we MUST try to follow all He requires of us. Knowing the contents of the heart will determine the truth of our desire to love and obey Him and not by what we say! In the scriptures, Jesus makes it clear what He expects of us even if we do not know Him personally. We do not have the liberty to accept or reject specific teachings of God so that the beliefs of others might be followed. God makes sure we understand the consequences of our actions, as recorded in 1 Corinthians.

Corinthians 1:19-21

¹⁹ For it is written, I will destroy the wisdom of the wise, and will bring to nothing the understanding of the prudent.
²⁰ Where is the wise? where is the scribe? where is the disputer of this world? hath not God made foolish the wisdom of this world?
²¹ For after that in the wisdom of God the world by wisdom knew not God, it pleased God by the foolishness of preaching to save them that believe.

I discovered during the intimate moments of loving God that we cannot know Him until He pursues us first based on the true humbling nature of our souls! God first draws us unto Himself. He does this AFTER searching our hearts to see if we genuinely want to know Him, or He knows that we can yet be converted. We might say we want to follow him or be one with him with our mouths, but our hearts are far away. Therefore, God searches the heart of all to determine the truth of what we say. Once God has established our level of truth, He seeks out those who are willing to serve Him! Once He has made Himself known to us, we are set out on a different path. We are introduced to a way of knowing God as He prepares our hearts to love Him. We soon come to know that nothing in life is more important than entering the presence of the LORD God. To find God, we must seek His presence fervently!

We must run HARD. We must THIRST for His truths. Our only goal, or objective, is to "LISTEN, HEAR, and OBEY." Search the scriptures below and review the requirements and instructions provided by the LORD. There is no room for personal bias. God expects our commitment and obedience. Just doing "good" among men is not the answer. The enemy of God, the devil, is seeking ALL that will sacrifice their desire to follow God and receive "goodness" offered from an evil source. Know that the devil presents goodness as righteousness. The soul not truly converted to listening, hearing, and obeying the LORD will remain open to the voice of evil. This is especially true if there is a self-gain to such a one.

> *He that is of God heareth God's words: ye therefore hear them not, because ye are not of God. ~ John 8:47*

When following God, we must leave behind our concerns and needs and trust that God knows what is best. We do not need to know the details of our path as we go forward. We only need to be persuaded and know that we are genuinely following the LORD! Reaching this goal allows our lives to surrender into God's hands regardless of our obstacles. We trust and believe that He will always work on our behalf. We NEVER doubt Him. We trust and obey! The scriptures below confirm what is required of us as true Christians. This understanding comes from *Resting in the Presence of the LORD*. Please carefully read and "Live" the scriptures below. To Live the scriptures is a process whereby you apply the words to your personal life to determine if your reading applies to you. In other words, you become a character in the story as you seek the face of the LORD! If you truthfully seek God with all your soul, He will respond. At the end of this process, you will know if you need to seek a deeper understanding or personal relationship with Almighty God. Be blessed as you travel on this sacred road:

> *It repenteth me that I have set up Saul to be king: for he is turned back from following me, and hath not performed my commandments. And it grieved Samuel; and he cried unto the LORD all night. ~ 1 Samuel 15:11*

> *And he saith unto them, Follow me, and I will make you fishers of men. ~ Matthew 4:19*

But Jesus said unto him, Follow me; and let the dead bury their dead. ~ Matthew 8:22

And as Jesus passed forth from thence, he saw a man, named Matthew, sitting at the receipt of custom: and he saith unto him, Follow me. And he arose and followed him. ~ Matthew 9:9

Then said Jesus unto his disciples, If any man will come after me, let him deny himself, and take up his cross, and follow me. ~ Matthew 16:24

Jesus said unto him, If thou wilt be perfect, go and sell that thou hast, and give to the poor, and thou shalt have treasure in heaven: and come and follow me. ~ Matthew 19:21

And Jesus said unto them, Verily I say unto you, That ye which have followed me, in the regeneration when the Son of man shall sit in the throne of his glory, ye also shall sit upon twelve thrones, judging the twelve tribes of Israel. ~ Matthew 19:28

² And he sent them to preach the kingdom of God, and to heal the sick.

³ And he said unto them, Take nothing for your journey, neither staves, nor scrip, neither bread, neither money; neither have two coats apiece. ~ Luke 9:2-3

[24] For whosoever will save his life shall lose it: but whosoever will lose his life for my sake, the same shall save it.

[25] For what is a man advantaged, if he gain the whole world, and lose himself, or be cast away?

[26] For whosoever shall be ashamed of me and of my words, of him shall the Son of man be ashamed, when he shall come in his own glory, and in his Father's, and of the holy angels. ~ Luke 9:24-26

[59] And he said unto another, Follow me. But he said, Lord, suffer me first to go and bury my father.

[60] Jesus said unto him, Let the dead bury their dead: but go thou and preach the kingdom of God. ~ Luke 9:59-60

So likewise, whosoever he be of you that forsaketh not all that he hath, he cannot be my disciple. ~ Luke 14:33

Then spake Jesus again unto them, saying, I am the light of the world: he that followeth me shall not walk in darkness, but shall have the light of life. ~ John 8:12

So Jesus was saying to the Jews who had believed Him, "If you abide in My word [continually obeying My teachings and living in accordance with them, then] you are truly My disciples. ~ John 8:31 (AMP)

My sheep hear my voice, and I know them, and they follow me: ~ John 10:27

If any man serve me, let him follow me; and where I am, there shall also my servant be: if any man serve me, him will my Father honour. ~ John 12:26

By this shall all men know that ye are my disciples, if ye have love one to another. ~ John 13:35

17 For the flesh lusteth against the Spirit, and the Spirit against the flesh: and these are contrary the one to the other: so that ye cannot do the things that ye would.

18 But if ye be led of the Spirit, ye are not under the law.

¹⁹ Now the works of the flesh are manifest, which are these; Adultery, fornication, uncleanness, lasciviousness,

²⁰ Idolatry, witchcraft, hatred, variance, emulations, wrath, strife, seditions, heresies,

²¹ Envyings, murders, drunkenness, revellings, and such like: of the which I tell you before, as I have also told you in time past, that they which do such things shall not inherit the kingdom of God. ~ Galatians 5:17-21

He that committeth sin is of the devil; for the devil sinneth from the beginning. For this purpose the Son of God was manifested, that he might destroy the works of the devil. ~ 1 John 3:8

In this the children of God are manifest, and the children of the devil: whosoever doeth not righteousness is not of God, neither he that loveth not his brother. ~ 1 John 3:10

Jesus said unto him, Thou shalt love the Lord thy God with all thy heart, and with all thy soul, and with all thy mind. ~ Matthew 22:37

And he answering said, Thou shalt love the Lord thy God with all thy heart, and with all thy soul, and with all thy strength, and with all thy mind; and thy neighbour as thyself. ~ Luke 10:27

When reading and *"living"* the referenced scriptures, it becomes crystal clear of the expectations of our Lord and Savior Jesus Christ of what it takes to obey and follow Him. There are no exceptions. At the guidance of the enemy of God, the world has watered down the requirements of love and obedience to just being good and following our own version of Christianity. Satan has convinced many that to follow our LORD and Savior as commanded is to live within a cult! Satan has perpetuated the belief that we alone should control our bodies and minds and not be subjected to what God has to say! All of this is with the knowledge that Satan is already in control and manipulating every thought.

It is essential to realize that Satan mimics the steps of God **almost** to perfection. He has used false followers to act against the will of God. Their actions, taken in God's name, have been proven to be cultish. As a result, faithful obedience to our God is viewed negatively. To summarize, when faithful followers of God Almighty live a life according to the scriptures referenced, they are most often considered as conspiracy theorists or following evil created by the devil himself!

Evil is glorified while minimizing the fact that it is a pathway to hell or diminishing what it means to be confined to Hell! The devil has orchestrated many ways for humankind to enter hell. Unfortunately, not everyone believes that the devil is real! I personally know that the devil exists. Again, my understanding is based on the divine revelation of the spiritual realm by the LORD and personal visits of evil forces as allowed by the LORD! God has provided revelation of His truths and the lies of Satan.

The devil can present himself to us in many ways:

1. He can appear in his own name to those who believe and know who he is.

2. He can possess the body of one who is filled with sin.

3. He can deceive us through illnesses.

4. Abominable sexual sin allows evil to control our thoughts and our flesh.

5. False religion enables Satan to feed lies into the minds of those who reject the truths of righteousness.

6. Material possessions valued more than God give access to evil; God must guard riches and fame.

7. Rebellion against the will of God is rooted in witchcraft and evil. This often leads to demonic possession.

8. Personal intellectual reliance on self rather than obeying the leading of God Almighty is evil. Our intellect is often used to camouflage Satan's lies.

9. Witchcraft and idol worship is directly against God the Father and the Holy Ghost.

10. Visiting psychic mediums is evil in the sight of God.

11. Additionally, the scriptures highlight that the devil captures an ignorant heart, unaware that he truly exists.

12. Liars are evil and those that spread lies are also under the will of evil.

And that they may recover themselves out of the snare of the devil, who are taken captive by him at his will. ~ 2 Timothy 2:26

He that committeth sin is of the devil; for the devil sinneth from the beginning. For this purpose the Son of God was manifested, that he might destroy the works of the devil. ~ 1 John 3:8

> *In this the children of God are manifest, and the children of the devil: whosoever doeth not righteousness is not of God, neither he that loveth not his brother. ~ 1 John 3:10*

If one can accept the scriptures outlined so far as truth, there should be no doubt in the heart of anyone who wants to truly follow God that He demands righteous living from His followers. The LORD is clear. There must be no one in our lives that we place before Him at any time:

> *Jesus said unto him, Thou shalt love the Lord thy God with all thy heart, and with all thy soul, and with all thy mind. ~ Matthew 22:37*

> *And thou shalt love the Lord thy God with all thy heart, and with all thy soul, and with all thy mind, and with all thy strength: this is the first commandment. ~ Mark 12:30*

> *And he answering said, Thou shalt love the Lord thy God with all thy heart, and with all thy soul, and with all thy strength, and with all thy mind; and thy neighbour as thyself. ~ Luke 10:27*

My dear friends, readers, and fellow Christians, please refrain from leaning on your own understanding of the relevance of the words written. The scriptures are included here for your review and analysis without comments from me. Therefore, be led by the very words of God! To do nothing is no longer an option. Assume for a moment my words are valid, and the LORD is truly calling for a change in our hearts. If so, we are all held accountable for our actions from now on. There is so much more I want to say; therefore, I remain available to anyone who desires more details. The LORD is calling for change that begins in our hearts. May God guide you on your journey to the absolute truth of the wisdom and divine revelations of God.

Scripturally, 3/4 of the Christian world is operating without Almighty God. The scriptures presented have clearly demonstrated to us how He feels about our sinfulness. Please read the complete chapter of 2 Peter for full accountability. We highlight here most of this chapter:

2 Peter 2:4-22

⁴ For if God spared not the angels that sinned, but cast them down to hell, and delivered them into chains of darkness, to be reserved unto judgment;

⁵ And spared not the old world, but saved Noah the eighth person, a preacher of righteousness, bringing in the flood upon the world of the ungodly;

⁶ And turning the cities of Sodom and Gomorrha into ashes condemned them with an overthrow, making them an ensample unto those that after should live ungodly;

⁷ And delivered just Lot, vexed with the filthy conversation of the wicked:

⁸ (For that righteous man dwelling among them, in seeing and hearing, vexed his righteous soul from day to day with their unlawful deeds;)

⁹ The Lord knoweth how to deliver the godly out of temptations and to reserve the unjust unto the day of judgment to be punished:

¹⁰ But chiefly them that walk after the flesh in the lust of uncleanness, and despise government. Presumptuous are they, selfwilled, they are not afraid to speak evil of dignities.

¹¹ Whereas angels, which are greater in power and might, bring not railing accusation against them before the Lord.

¹² But these, as natural brute beasts, made to be taken and destroyed, speak evil of the things that they understand not; and shall utterly perish in their own corruption;

¹³ And shall receive the reward of unrighteousness, as they that count it pleasure to riot in the day time. Spots they are and blemishes, sporting themselves with their own deceivings while they feast with you;

¹⁴ Having eyes full of adultery, and that cannot cease from sin; beguiling unstable souls: an heart they have exercised with covetous practices; cursed children:

¹⁵ Which have forsaken the right way, and are gone astray, following the way of Balaam the son of Bosor, who loved the wages of unrighteousness;

¹⁶ But was rebuked for his iniquity: the dumb ass speaking with man's voice forbad the madness of the prophet.

¹⁷ These are wells without water, clouds that are carried with a tempest; to whom the mist of darkness is reserved for ever.

¹⁸ For when they speak great swelling words of vanity, they allure through the lusts of the flesh, through much wantonness, those that were clean escaped from them who live in error.

¹⁹ While they promise them liberty, they themselves are the servants of corruption: for of whom a man is overcome, of the same is he brought in bondage.

> *²⁰ For if after they have escaped the pollutions of the world through the knowledge of the Lord and Saviour Jesus Christ, they are again entangled therein, and overcome, the latter end is worse with them than the beginning.*
>
> *²¹ For it had been better for them not to have known the way of righteousness, than, after they have known it, to turn from the holy commandment delivered unto them.*
>
> *²² But it is happened unto them according to the true proverb, The dog is turned to his own vomit again; and the sow that was washed to her wallowing in the mire.*

God has charged me to deliver to the Christian world His message that ¾ of the Christian world is on the way to Hell and does not know it. As hard as this statement is to accept for many, it remains true. I repeat it here as I want all to grasp this as an urgent message for change from our LORD. I repeat… He is calling us to change! This request is supported by scripture, specifically in three places in the Holy Scriptures of the Bible, but I will elaborate here only on Mathew 13.

Matthew 13:3-23

³ And he spake many things unto them in parables, saying, Behold, a sower went forth to sow;

⁴ And when he sowed, some seeds fell by the way side, and the fowls came and devoured them up: ⁵ Some fell upon stony places, where they had not much earth: and forthwith they sprung up, because they had no deepness of earth:

⁶ And when the sun was up, they were scorched; and because they had no root, they withered away.

⁷ And some fell among thorns; and the thorns sprung up, and choked them:

⁸ But other fell into good ground, and brought forth fruit, some an hundredfold, some sixtyfold, some thirtyfold.

⁹ Who hath ears to hear, let him hear.

¹⁰ And the disciples came, and said unto him, Why speakest thou unto them in parables?

¹¹ He answered and said unto them, Because it is given unto you to know the mysteries of the kingdom of heaven, but to them it is not given.

¹² For whosoever hath, to him shall be given, and he shall have more abundance: but whosoever hath not, from him shall be taken away even that he hath.

¹³ Therefore speak I to them in parables: because they seeing see not; and hearing they hear not, neither do they understand.

¹⁴ And in them is fulfilled the prophecy of Esaias, which saith, By hearing ye shall hear, and shall not understand; and seeing ye shall see, and shall not perceive:

¹⁵ For this people's heart is waxed gross, and their ears are dull of hearing, and their eyes they have closed; lest at any time they should see with their eyes and hear with their ears, and should understand with their heart, and should be converted, and I should heal them.

¹⁶ But blessed are your eyes, for they see: and your ears, for they hear.

¹⁷ For verily I say unto you, That many prophets and righteous men have desired to see those things which ye see, and have not seen them; and to hear those things which ye hear, and have not heard them.

¹⁸ Hear ye therefore the parable of the sower.

¹⁹ When any one heareth the word of the kingdom, and understandeth it not, then cometh the wicked one, and catcheth away that which was sown in his heart. This is he which received seed by the way side.

²⁰ But he that received the seed into stony places, the same is he that heareth the word, and anon with joy receiveth it;

> *²¹ Yet hath he not root in himself, but dureth for a while: for when tribulation or persecution ariseth because of the word, by and by he is offended.*
>
> *²² He also that received seed among the thorns is he that heareth the word; and the care of this world, and the deceitfulness of riches, choke the word, and he becometh unfruitful.*
>
> *²³ But he that received seed into the good ground is he that heareth the word, and understandeth it; which also beareth fruit, and bringeth forth, some an hundredfold, some sixty, some thirty.*

Regarding this critical subject, a condensed explanation of the revelation shows the crucial need for us all to perfect our personal relationship with the LORD. God has now given me scriptural proof of this divine revelation, as recorded in Mathew 13. However, He initially sent me out to announce, teach, and declare this truth when I had nothing to rely on except His Spoken Word! Unfortunately, the parable found in Mathew 13 is often referenced by teachers and theologians and explained in various ways. Yet, I have never heard the correct meaning as God Himself describes. Each time I attempt to correct this false understanding or explain what God is saying, I am viewed as a radical leftwing person pushing a theory contrary to the holy scriptures. I am not believed, even after sharing my testimony to explain that these revelations have been presented to me by the LORD. Most often, they then tell me God does not speak! Many say if God wanted them to know this meaning, it would have been a part of the scriptures. IT IS IN THE SCRIPTURES! Immediately after the scriptures in Mathew 13, as stated by Jesus in His own words, it becomes clear that not everyone would understand His saying. Mathew 13:9 explicitly states that those with an ear to hear should hear! Do you have an ear to hear what God is saying? Unfortunately, to reject the Wisdom of God and rely on our own understanding is to reject God Himself. This is a critical mistake that is prominent today within the body of Christ.

Jesus spoke of many mysteries within scripture that alluded to the spiritual understanding of those who heard Him teach and the current generation. He explained that His mysteries are not intended for those who are not His followers or those with no relationship with Him. Read the words for yourself. Please do not believe me. I have included the scripture herein to further your understanding. See Mathew 13:13-17 above.

God said that ¾ of the Christian world is on the way to hell and does not even know it! The parable breaks down into four categories, with three in dangerous positions. Let's examine all four categories that Jesus exposed.

Category 1:

> *¹⁹ When any one heareth the word of the kingdom, and understandeth it not, then cometh the wicked one, and catcheth away that which was sown in his heart. This is he which received seed by the way side.*

1. Verse 19 declares several truths you must accept to understand the revelation. According to Jesus, those who fall into this category are lost and on the way to hell and do not know it.

2. This portion of the parable speaks to those who hear the Word but do not understand it. It does not penetrate the heart or soul as truth from God. Such a one cannot hold onto the Word received. The heart cannot hold onto any truths as they were only naturally understood or on the surface and not rooted in the heart as absolute truth from the LORD.

3. Anyone who hears the Word of God and fails to understand what is "literally" being said is NOT in a good place. This

demonstrates that one can read the scriptures yet not comprehend the spiritual lesson. It confirms that an intellectual understanding of the Scriptures is not sufficient to know the teachings of our Lord Jesus Christ.

4. The scriptures state that when one utterly fails to understand the words, the devil comes along and removes any understanding that could have been gained.

Category 2:

> [20] But he that received the seed into stony places, the same is he that heareth the word, and anon with joy receiveth it;
>
> [21] Yet hath he not root in himself, but dureth for a while: for when tribulation or persecution ariseth because of the word, by and by he is offended.

1. Category 2, as stated in verses 20 and 21 above, shows the path of those who fail to follow the path of the LORD. They are on the way to Hell and do not know it.

2. The parable refers to the seed that falls in stony places. God says if the heart is not yet surrendered to Him, it cannot hold onto any truths received. Initially, such a one is excited and

happy about the teachings received, but quickly abandons the belief once held! It is not good to have a "stony" heart.

3. The Word fails to materialize within the soul since it falls into a "stony" heart NOT submitted unto the Lord. It will endure temporarily until persecution or tribulation comes along. Because there is no union with the Lord, such a one cannot hold onto the truths received.

4. Those in this category soon follow false teachings or rely upon their intellect and believe it is ok to do so.

Category 3:

[22] He also that received seed among the thorns is he that heareth the word; and the care of this world, and the deceitfulness of riches, choke the word, and he becometh unfruitful.

1. Category 3 is described in verse 22 above. So many false Christians fall into this category. The people here are on the way to hell and don't know it, thus saith the LORD.

2. They have heard the Word and believe what they have heard, but they try to reconcile the natural teachings of the world with the teachings of Jesus Christ.

3. These individuals are willing to compromise on what they claim to believe for the sake of riches or acceptance by others.

4. They cannot hold onto scriptural truths they claim are real. They allow others to contaminate their beliefs and cannot stand for the truth or have an uncompromised testimony of faith. They, too, are lost, according to God.

Category 4:

> *²³ But he that received seed into the good ground is he that heareth the word, and understandeth it; which also beareth fruit, and bringeth forth, some an hundredfold, some sixty, some thirty.*

1. Considering all four categories, this is undoubtedly the most advantageous. Here, the struggle and life of a true believer unfold as they navigate this natural world. Here we find those who have overcome the last three categories outlined. This fourth category is safe according to the teachings of Jesus Christ.

2. The Word of God is heard and received within the soul. It is planted deep within the heart, but they must endure until

the end.

3. The Word received is understood and believed as actual lessons taught by the LORD God,

4. Due to unfailing faith and belief in the teachings of the LORD, such a one listens, follows, and obeys. They can inspire others to believe in and follow those who genuinely stand for God. Much fruit is produced and sown into the lives of others.

The task for us all is to humble ourselves before the great "I AM" and repent of all things. We often do not know what to say or how to pray. Becoming intimate with "I AM" is a spiritual journey that can only be realized or begun in absolute surrender to God. With me, it started with love and a desire to understand what lay before me. I continuously prayed that God would "change me and dissect my soul." I labored months before God, seeking Him and His ways. I knew that something within me had to be changed, even though I did not know what to do.

At this point in my experience, I did not have the correct understanding of who God Is! It was through the dissection of my soul that my knowledge developed. I now know that it was and still is the will of God for me to enter His Presence and stay there! This is where ALL learning takes place.

~ 11 ~

The Beginning Before the Beginning

> [16] *This I say then, Walk in the Spirit, and ye shall not fulfil the lust of the flesh.*
> [17] *For the flesh lusteth against the Spirit, and the Spirit against the flesh: and these are contrary the one to the other: so that ye cannot do the things that ye would.* ~ *Galatians 5:16-17*

Many scientific experts have given most of the world an alternate understanding of how our universe came to be. This, too, lets me know that such people have not yet met Jesus Christ, the Living Son of God! It is often said that we do not know what we don't know. This is so true. How can I explain what I do know when there are so many obstacles to the belief and understanding of the reality of such a righteous God? Jesus made it clear to Nicodemus that there are spiritual things that leaders should know but do not.

John 3:10-12

¹⁰ Jesus answered and said unto him, Art thou a master of Israel, and knowest not these things?

¹¹ Verily, verily, I say unto thee, We speak that we do know, and testify that we have seen; and ye receive not our witness.

¹² If I have told you earthly things, and ye believe not, how shall ye believe, if I tell you of heavenly things?

Jesus made it very simple to understand while instructing Nicodemus about who He really is in the world. He knew that the world would not understand, even though His heart was broken!

While standing in the presence of the LORD God Almighty, loving Him with my whole heart, I was introduced to the most amazing truths by my LORD. Within this book I tell you about some of these revelations and ask that you look to the Great "I AM" for clarification!

Romans 1:16-23

[16] *For I am not ashamed of the gospel of Christ: for it is the power of God unto salvation to every one that believeth; to the Jew first, and also to the Greek.*
[17] *For therein is the righteousness of God*

revealed from faith to faith: as it is written, The just shall live by faith.
[18] *For the wrath of God is revealed from heaven against all ungodliness and unrighteousness of men, who hold the truth in unrighteousness;*
[19] *Because that which may be known of God is manifest in them; for God hath shewed it unto them.*
[20] *For the invisible things of him from the creation of the world are clearly seen, being understood by the things that are made, even his eternal power and Godhead; so that they are without excuse:*
[21] *Because that, when they knew God, they glorified him not as God, neither were thankful; but became vain in their imaginations, and their foolish heart was darkened.*
[22] *Professing themselves to be wise, they became fools,*
[23] *And changed the glory of the uncorruptible God into an image made like to corruptible*

> *man, and to birds, and fourfooted beasts, and creeping things.*

The following revelation provides details of the spiritual world occurrences before the scriptures contained in the book of Genesis, where most believers claim the world began. God has shown me the truth of the beginning of the world and mankind! Realizing that there might even be more than I know, I record here what I do know. Also, the revelation I am about to discuss will lead you to additional revelations that appear at the beginning of biblical Genesis, and there is yet more to come. I pray you will truly seek the face of God regarding all stated revelations.

The true facts related to life on earth and to the book of Genesis begin at the conclusion of a spiritual battle between the LORD GOD and Lucifer. All the Heavenly Hosts were included in the battle due to the confusion caused by Lucifer. The scriptures inform us that Lucifer was cast down from Heaven to Earth due to his pride. God has also shown me that jealousy was also a significant factor involved! The operation of humankind was established at this time. Understanding this section requires you not to lean on your own understanding. AMEN.

The First Beginning:

Before anything in the universe existed, the LORD God Almighty lived. Nothing was created or made until He created it. His Holy Dwelling place was in Heaven above all that He had made. The sun, moon, and stars occupied a space nearby and were introduced to the world during the second beginning. Within this Holy Space, God dwelled after creating a host of angelic beings that served Him alone and carried out His plans for the peaceful existence of all of creation.

God the Creator existed then, and now, as all-knowing! Nothing existed before Him, and without His knowledge, no actions were taken without His approval. He could see all the things in the universe that He had created. The mindset of all angelic beings was always known. Just as every thought and intent of the heart of man today is always known!

Lucifer was a beautiful angelic being created by God, demanding constant praise and attention. He required all other heavenly beings to cherish and admire his every action. He was filled with pride and selfishness! He yearned for greater power and sought to be wise and in control of all things. He wanted to be God. As a spiritual being, Lucifer could personify himself as male or female as well as animals. As a female, he longed to be the daily delight and companion of the LORD GOD. As the Holy Ghost already occupied this role, God rejected him![1] In his anger and revenge for being rejected by God, he sought the companionship of the Holy Ghost directly instead of the LORD, presenting himself as female! This adjustment was to anger the LORD. This combination alone was abominable to God and to the Holy Ghost, so he was again rejected! This so angered Lucifer that he started recruiting other angels to join him in seditiously defying God to overturn the peaceful order of the spiritual world to allow himself to be greater than or equal to God.[2]

The greatest battle and insurrection this world have ever known occurred *"in the beginning before the beginning."* The details of the outcome of this spiritual battle are outlined in Genesis Chapter 1. Here, the Lord outlined the creation of the natural world as we know it today and the ongoing spiritual

---

[1] See Proverbs 8 for clarification of the role of the Holy Ghost and the intimate relationship with God Almighty.
[2] This was the first act of sedition in the world as performed by Lucifer. He would ultimately use this same technique to cause mankind to rebel against authority and pull many souls further into sin!

world order. God Almighty won the battle. The aftermath of this spiritual war begins with Genesis Chapter 1 as the 2nd beginning.

The Second Beginning: The Truth about the fallen angels or spirits:

After the defeat of Lucifer, the second part of creation begins in the book of Genesis. Here, we can see God's great love and attention given even to those who rebelled against Him. As Creator of the spiritual world, God created a home even for those who tried to overthrow His Kingdom. You see, no matter what, He was still God of ALL and unwilling to abandon any of His creation! He truly was and is a loving God to all! Let's examine the scriptures within Genesis line by line.

> *In the beginning, God created the heaven and the earth.* ~ Genesis 1:1

This creation was after Lucifer and his angelic followers were cast out of the Holy Dwelling Place of God.

> *And the earth was without form, and void; and darkness was upon the face of the deep.*

> *And the Spirit of God moved upon the face of the waters. ~ Genesis 1:2*

Lucifer and his followers are referred to as "darkness," and called "deep" or water. Water is black and has no form, and again Lucifer tried to maintain control over these fallen spirits. However, God Himself moved over the face of these dark evil waters to demonstrate that He alone is God!

> *And God said, Let there be light: and there was light. ~ Genesis 1:3*

As a forgiving God, another chance to be with God was offered to all those who had listened to Lucifer's lies and rebelled with him against God. Every spiritual being was allowed to stay with God and be a part of His everlasting light or become forever darkness and follow Lucifer!

> *And God saw the light, that it was good: and God divided the light from the darkness. ~ Genesis 1:4*

God was pleased to see 2/3 of the angelic host desired to remain as light and stay within His presence. Therefore, He divided these beings of light from the darkness that had rebelled with Lucifer.

> *And God called the light Day, and the darkness he called Night. And the evening and the morning were the first day. ~ Genesis 1:5[3]*

The presence of God is powerful during the daylight hours since He is light! His watchful eyes see and protect us all. Evil is apparent more keenly during the night hours of darkness!

> *And God said, Let there be a firmament in the midst of the waters, and let it divide the waters from the waters. ~ Genesis 1:6*

In preparing a place for the fallen spirits to live away from Him and the Heavenly Hosts, God created a firmament between the waters (spirits) above and the waters (dark spirits) remaining on earth. The firmament is that part of the sky above that we can see with our natural eyes.

---

[3] Here too lies another great mystery that will be revealed by the LORD at the appropriate time. Amen.

> *And God made the firmament and divided the waters which were under the firmament from the waters which were above the firmament: and it was so. ~ Genesis 1:7*

The waters, or deep, are evil spirits! In fact, all water is spirit and validated throughout the scriptures.

> *And God called the firmament Heaven. And the evening and the morning were the second day. ~ Genesis 1:8*

> *And God said, Let the waters under the heaven be gathered together unto one place, and let the dry land appear: and it was so. ~ Genesis 1:9*

The waters under the Heaven created by God were the rebellious dark spirits that followed Lucifer and fought against God. In fact, God rolled them all into "one place" to become their habitation and their forever home until God permanently deals with them!

> *And God called the dry land Earth; and the gathering together of the waters called he Seas: and God saw that it was good. ~ Genesis 1:10*

The exposed land, when God gathered the dark waters together (evil spirits), He called Earth. This is the same Earth upon which we now live! All the waters gathered were called Seas. These are the same seas we have today, and they have become playgrounds for the world! They represent spiritual darkness and evil spirits! In fact, God commanded the seas that this was a boundary that they were not to cross.

The dry land that He called Earth was once connected to the sea and contains an evil foundation! At some point, the sea and the land called Earth will reunite! If we consider the devastation that is now appearing worldwide, we can see this spiritual reunion being manifested before our eyes daily. This highlights the occurrence of mighty floods, hurricanes, and tornadoes that remain inexplicable and unsolved.

All these things occur as resultant damage stemming from the battle between good and evil, between God and Satan! Understanding all that has happened in the world since the Beginning battle makes the excellent spiritual strategy provided by the LORD for our world an incredible reality. After giving the Earth and Sea His commands, God created Man, which continues to be a part of His Strategic Master Plan. Proverbs 8, mentioned previously and stated below, thoroughly explains that **Wisdom** (also known as the Holy Ghost) is the holy counterpart of God and was with Him during *"The Beginning Before the Beginning"* before Lucifer tried to overthrow God or proposition the Holy Ghost!

Proverbs 8:22- 33

²² The LORD possessed me in the beginning of his way, before his works of old.
²³ I was set up from everlasting, from the beginning, or ever the earth was.
²⁴ When there were no depths, I was brought forth; when there were no fountains abounding with water.
²⁵ Before the mountains were settled, before the hills was I brought forth:

²⁶ While as yet he had not made the earth, nor the fields, nor the highest part of the dust of the world.
²⁷ When he prepared the heavens, I was there: when he set a compass upon the face of the depth:
²⁸ When he established the clouds above: when he strengthened the fountains of the deep:
²⁹ When he gave to the sea his decree, that the waters should not pass his commandment: when he appointed the foundations of the earth:

³⁰ Then I was by him, as one brought up with him: and I was daily his delight, rejoicing always before him;
³¹ Rejoicing in the habitable part of his earth; and my delights were with the sons of men.
³² Now therefore hearken unto me, O ye children: for blessed are they that keep my ways.
³³ Hear instruction, and be wise, and refuse it not.

The world does not yet understand the essence of water. This Satan is counting on. 99% of all things made in the world utilize water. Due to our ignorance, we can easily become confused or be led to operate outside God's will. We become very excited when we hear of new inventions and strive to be the best in understanding how to incorporate them into our lives.

Let's take a strong look at NASA. They have discovered water within rocks taken from Outer Space and placed significant inferences on what this could mean for future explorations. Astronomers have reported studies related to the discovery of a 12-billion-year-old body of water floating in space. [4] I am not a Scientist, so I can only say that the Astronomers and scientists seem clueless about the nature of the water they've found. I ask them to submit themselves before God in prayer so that they might be given the correct discernment of what they have discovered. This again proves that Mankind has discounted the truth and recognition that God Almighty created it all.

---

[4] Further details of this study can be found on this website: Unilad, https://www.unilad.com/technology/space/water-space-quasar-nasa-explained- 923559-20240320

~ 11 ~

The Sea Is the Assigned Home of Lucifer/Satan/Demons

Water, all water, is spirit! Therefore, we need to know which spirit we are dealing with in life. It is either Holy or unholy. Also, know that there is a difference between the Holy Ghost and the Holy Spirit! The Spirit that refers to God, Jesus Christ, or the Holy Ghost alludes to the character, righteous nature, or Spirit of the Godhead. Man has been conditioned to interchange the term, Holy Spirit with the Holy Ghost, which is inaccurate according to the LORD! This error has allowed many to disavow even the existence of the Holy Ghost! The Holy Spirit is NOT a person, but rather, it describes or explains the type of spirit that dwells as a part of God the Father, the Holy Ghost, and Jesus Christ! The Holy Spirit decidedly helps us to see it as an attribute that is generated only by the LORD.

Let's look at some scripture references to better understand the essence of water according to the LORD. The righteousness of God is always presented:

A fountain of gardens, a well of living waters, and streams from Lebanon. ~ Song of Solomon 4:15

O LORD, the hope of Israel, all that forsake thee shall be ashamed, and they that depart from me shall be written in the earth, because they have forsaken the LORD, the fountain of living waters. ~ Jeremiah 17:13

And it shall be in that day, that living waters shall go out from Jerusalem; half of them toward the former sea, and half of them toward the hinder sea: in summer and in winter shall it be. ~ Zechariah 14:8

The ignorance of mankind is profound when exploring the spiritual realm. Not understanding the essence of the Sea and Earth, Mankind has allowed evil to prevail on earth!

Genesis 1:6-10

[6] And God said, Let there be a firmament in the midst of the waters, and let it divide the waters from the waters.
[7] And God made the firmament, and divided the waters which were under the firmament

from the waters which were above the firmament: and it was so.
⁸ And God called the firmament Heaven. And the evening and the morning were the second day.
⁹ And God said, Let the waters under the heaven be gathered together unto one place, and let the dry land appear: and it was so.
¹⁰ And God called the dry land Earth; and the gathering together of the waters called he Seas: and God saw that it was good.

And when Jesus had cried with a loud voice, he said, Father, into thy hands I commend my spirit: and having said thus, he gave up the ghost. ~ Luke 23:46

But one of the soldiers with a spear pierced his side, and forthwith came there out blood and water. ~ John 19:34

For my people have committed two evils; they have forsaken me the fountain of living waters, and hewed them out cisterns, broken cisterns, that can hold no water. ~ Jeremiah 2:13

Jesus answered and said unto her, If thou knewest the gift of God, and who it is that saith to thee, Give me to drink; thou wouldest have asked of him, and he would have given thee living water. ~ John 4:10

The woman saith unto him, Sir, thou hast nothing to draw with, and the well is deep: from whence then hast thou that living water? ~ John 4:11

He that believeth on me, as the scripture hath said, out of his belly shall flow rivers of living water. ~ John 7:38

The above scriptures that have been stated remain in plain view for all to see and I invite all "who have ears to hear and eyes to see"! As shown in Jeremiah 2:13 above, the current church has yet again abandoned the true teachings and understanding of the LORD by accepting false beliefs about God while following and believing the lies of His adversary! Resting in the Presence of the LORD is the only way to survive.

Take a close look at the practice of Baptism. It should not be a sprinkling but submerging of the entire body. Being confident that the heart is repentant and submitted unto God, such a one is saying to the enemy of God that he can fully be covered with the dark waters and stand strong in the end with no fear of the evil waters! It demonstrates the willingness to go under and come up bolder in Christ than before. However, the unrepentant evil heart will be drawn further into darkness with total submersion in the water. Amen.

I tell you without any doubt that the Sea as we know it is a bed of demonic spirits assigned there by God during the fall of Lucifer from Heaven. The book of Revelation confirms that, in the end, the sea will no longer exist.

<u>Revelation 21:1-8</u>

> *[1] And I saw a new heaven and a new earth: for the first heaven and the first earth were passed away; and there was no more sea.*
>
> *[2] And I John saw the holy city, new Jerusalem, coming down from God out of heaven, prepared as a bride adorned for her husband.*
>
> *[3] And I heard a great voice out of heaven saying, Behold, the tabernacle of God is with men, and he will dwell with them, and they shall be his people, and God himself shall be with them, and be their God.*
>
> *[4] And God shall wipe away all tears from their eyes; and there shall be no more death, neither sorrow, nor crying, neither shall there be any*

more pain: for the former things are passed away.

⁵ And he that sat upon the throne said, Behold, I make all things new. And he said unto me, Write: for these words are true and faithful.

⁶ And he said unto me, It is done. I am Alpha and Omega, the beginning and the end. I will give unto him that is athirst of the fountain of the water of life freely.

⁷ He that overcometh shall inherit all things; and I will be his God, and he shall be my son.

⁸ But the fearful, and unbelieving, and the abominable, and murderers, and whoremongers, and sorcerers, and idolaters, and all liars, shall have their part in the lake which burneth with fire and brimstone: which is the second death.

Throughout the scriptures, God makes it clear that He does not expect us to understand all He has done. He only asks that we listen to Him and obey! Unfortunately, mankind has followed the adversary of God instead. Currently, there are so many conspiracy theories circulating throughout the world, particularly in the Evangelical and political sectors. This was all planned by the adversary. The intent is that when the truths from God are revealed, they will quickly be seen as wild stories and false truths! Just as the enemy planted wild stories that Jesus

Christ could not be the Son of God or had not truly been risen from the dead by Father God. So it is with us today.

There is so much more that can be said or explained about Living Water as the actual Spirit of God, but unless one has been granted the Spiritual Discernment of God or has an ear to hear what thus saith the LORD, there is no hope of understanding. However, I am willing to explain more to those who wish to listen to the lessons of God that are documented in the Holy Scriptures and divinely instructed within this book. Amen.

Before leaving this subject, let's look briefly at more scriptures from the book of Revelation that clearly outline who and what the Sea is.

> *And before the throne there was a sea of glass like unto crystal: and in the midst of the throne, and round about the throne, were four beasts full of eyes before and behind. ~ Revelation 4:6*

> *And every creature which is in heaven, and on the earth, and under the earth, and such as are in the sea, and all that are in them, heard I saying, Blessing, and honour, and glory, and power, be unto him that sitteth upon the throne, and unto the Lamb for ever and ever.*
> *~ Revelation 5:13*

And after these things I saw four angels standing on the four corners of the earth, holding the four winds of the earth, that the wind should not blow on the earth, nor on the sea, nor on any tree. ~ Revelation 7:1

And I saw another angel ascending from the east, having the seal of the living God: and he cried with a loud voice to the four angels, to whom it was given to hurt the earth and the sea, ~ Revelation 7:2

Saying, Hurt not the earth, neither the sea, nor the trees, till we have sealed the servants of our God in their foreheads. ~ Revelation 7:3

And the second angel sounded, and as it were a great mountain burning with fire was cast into the sea: and the third part of the sea became blood; ~ Revelation 8:8

And the third part of the creatures which were in the sea, and had life, died; and the third part of the ships were destroyed. ~ Revelation 8:9

And he had in his hand a little book open: and he set his right foot upon the sea, and his left foot on the earth, ~ Revelation 10:2

And the angel which I saw stand upon the sea and upon the earth lifted up his hand to heaven, ~ *Revelation 10:5*

And sware by him that liveth for ever and ever, who created heaven, and the things that therein are, and the earth, and the things that therein are, and the sea, and the things which are therein, that there should be time no longer: ~ *Revelation 10:6*

And the voice which I heard from heaven spake unto me again, and said, Go and take the little book which is open in the hand of the angel which standeth upon the sea and upon the earth. ~ *Revelation 10:8*

Therefore rejoice, ye heavens, and ye that dwell in them. Woe to the inhabiters of the earth and of the sea! for the devil is come down unto you, having great wrath, because he knoweth that he hath but a short time. ~ *Revelation 12:12*

And I stood upon the sand of the sea, and saw a beast rise up out of the sea, having seven heads and ten horns, and upon his horns ten crowns, and upon his heads the name of blasphemy. ~ *Revelation 13:1*

Saying with a loud voice, Fear God, and give glory to him; for the hour of his judgment is come: and worship him that made heaven, and earth, and the sea, and the fountains of waters.
~ Revelation 14:7

And I saw as it were a sea of glass mingled with fire: and them that had gotten the victory over the beast, and over his image, and over his mark, and over the number of his name, stand on the sea of glass, having the harps of God.
~ Revelation 15:2

And the second angel poured out his vial upon the sea; and it became as the blood of a dead man: and every living soul died in the sea.
~ Revelation 16:3

For in one hour so great riches is come to nought. And every shipmaster, and all the company in ships, and sailors, and as many as trade by sea, stood afar off, ~ Revelation 18:17

And they cast dust on their heads, and cried, weeping and wailing, saying, Alas, alas, that great city, wherein were made rich all that had ships in the sea by reason of her costliness! for in one hour is she made desolate. ~ Revelation 18:19

And a mighty angel took up a stone like a great millstone, and cast it into the sea, saying, Thus with violence shall that great city Babylon be thrown down, and shall be found no more at all. ~ Revelation 18:21

And shall go out to deceive the nations which are in the four quarters of the earth, Gog and Magog, to gather them together to battle: the number of whom is as the sand of the sea. ~ Revelation 20:8

And the sea gave up the dead which were in it; and death and hell delivered up the dead which were in them: and they were judged every man according to their works. ~ Revelation 20:13

And I saw a new heaven and a new earth: for the first heaven and the first earth were passed away; and there was no more sea. ~ Revelation 21:1

May The LORD God Almighty

Have Mercy Upon Us All

~ 13 ~

Woman Is Hated by Satan

This revelation is HUGE if one understands how it relates to the existence of the Holy Ghost. Go back and reread the section of *"The Beginning Before the Beginning"* for added clarification. This is NOT science fiction! For a surety, Satan is angry at God and Woman. The enmity between woman and Satan began in the Garden of Eden. Know that God intends to strike another deadly blow to Satan using the hand of a woman! Because Satan does not know who will be used by God, he attempts to abuse all women along the way, just as he killed all boy babies as he tried to kill Jesus when He was born!

Who is the devil or Satan? It is essential to understand that another name for the Devil or Satan is "Serpent."

> *And the great dragon was cast out, that old serpent, called the Devil, and Satan, which deceiveth the whole world: he was cast out into the earth, and his angels were cast out with him. ~ Revelation 12:9*

He has deceived the whole world. Many, including Christians, have taken him into their homes as pets! The serpent, or snake that crawls on earth, is a product of the devil himself! It all boils down to some believing that everything on earth is good and comes from God. We need to discern what is of God and what is not!

Consider all the horrible things that are thrown at women today. These occurrences are not by accident. Most of this abuse begins during the early years of life for women. It can occur in the following ways:

- Physical or emotional abuse by a parent
- Bullying activities in school
- Sexual molestation by family members or close male friends
- Introduction to prostitution by those who have consistently abused women.
- Drug abuse and/or attempted suicide
- Refusal to allow women to become educated or strive for better life options.
- Black and Minority women are abused or attacked more than any other. Have you ever wondered why? This, too, is

a great mystery!

There are so many additional ways that women are abused that go beyond the list above. Evil attacks establish a pathway into the life of every woman from the very start of her life!

Parents play a critical part in the life of children from birth. Every child is born with an inherent knowledge of God! It is the responsibility of the parents to nourish and inspire this new soul in the existence and reality of the LORD God. It is crucial as the spiritual world is open and available for them to see, hear, and understand. This knowledge is critically important as it relates to females. The LORD will spiritually instruct parents who maintain an intimate relationship with God in raising such a child. If this spiritual relationship is not nourished, it can be lost forever! The good news is that God can protect and keep this soul connected to Him as He alone guides the future ways. Such was the case with Samuel when God called him as a child and spiritually led him through life. Please protect your children by wholeheartedly loving God first and then your child.

Satan entices the souls of men and women to follow his ways by granting lustful ways and untold riches of success. Men are always to protect women from the wiles of the devil, and women have an unspoken and hidden pathway to the heart of God that is readily available to all and allows the Lord to know their hearts. What great mysteries lie within this statement that God desires all women to discover!

~ 14 ~

The Holy Ghost is the Female Counterpart of the LORD

I know many of you are highly skeptical of my statement regarding the Holy Ghost. Yet, I am required to tell you what I have been commanded to say. Remembering that Lucifer was intensely jealous of the Holy Ghost, who is the Counterpart of God, it is not surprising that he also tried to defame Eve and all women to try and ridicule our LORD!

Lucifer wanted more power and was willing to secure it by any means whatsoever. He was not content to be a follower of the LORD and therefore set out to declare himself as God. As stated in the section of the *"Beginning Before the Beginning"*, he also tried to seduce the Holy Ghost! This was the ultimate test of rebellion and betrayal before God, and he was therefore defeated in battle by God and thrown out of Heaven for good.

Know also that the Holy Ghost, Wisdom, and Tree of Life are all the same! You cannot know one without understanding the relationship of all three and how they interact with Father God.

Consider the scriptures below and view them while considering the truth of who the Holy Ghost is, considering this revelation of the true identity of the Holy Ghost:

<u>Wisdom and the Holy Ghost</u>

<u>Proverbs 1:2-33</u>

² To know wisdom and instruction; to perceive the words of understanding;
³ To receive the instruction of wisdom, justice, and judgment, and equity;
⁴ To give subtilty to the simple, to the young man knowledge and discretion.
⁵ A wise man will hear, and will increase learning; and a man of understanding shall attain unto wise counsels:
⁶ To understand a proverb, and the interpretation; the words of the wise, and their dark sayings.
⁷ The fear of the LORD is the beginning of knowledge: but fools despise wisdom and instruction.
⁸ My son, hear the instruction of thy father, and forsake not the law of thy mother:
⁹ For they shall be an ornament of grace unto thy head, and chains about thy neck.
¹⁰ My son, if sinners entice thee, consent thou not.

[11] *If they say, Come with us, let us lay wait for blood, let us lurk privily for the innocent without cause:*

[12] *Let us swallow them up alive as the grave; and whole, as those that go down into the pit:*

[13] *We shall find all precious substance, we shall fill our houses with spoil:*

[14] *Cast in thy lot among us; let us all have one purse:*

[15] *My son, walk not thou in the way with them; refrain thy foot from their path:*

[16] *For their feet run to evil, and make haste to shed blood.*

[17] *Surely in vain, the net is spread in the sight of any bird.*

[18] *And they lay wait for their own blood; they lurk privily for their own lives.*

[19] *So are the ways of every one that is greedy of gain; which taketh away the life of the owners thereof.*

[20] *Wisdom crieth without; she uttereth her voice in the streets:*

[21] *She crieth in the chief place of concourse, in the openings of the gates: in the city she uttereth her words, saying,*

[22] *How long, ye simple ones, will ye love simplicity? and the scorners delight in their scorning, and fools hate knowledge?*

[23] *Turn you at my reproof: behold, I will pour out my spirit unto you, I will make known my words unto you.*

²⁴ Because I have called, and ye refused; I have stretched out my hand, and no man regarded;
²⁵ But ye have set at nought all my counsel, and would none of my reproof:
²⁶ I also will laugh at your calamity; I will mock when your fear cometh;
²⁷ When your fear cometh as desolation, and your destruction cometh as a whirlwind; when distress and anguish cometh upon you.
²⁸ Then shall they call upon me, but I will not answer; they shall seek me early, but they shall not find me:
²⁹ For that they hated knowledge, and did not choose the fear of the LORD:
³⁰ They would none of my counsel: they despised all my reproof.
³¹ Therefore shall they eat of the fruit of their own way, and be filled with their own devices.
³² For the turning away of the simple shall slay them, and the prosperity of fools shall destroy them.
³³ But whoso hearkeneth unto me shall dwell safely, and shall be quiet from fear of evil.

Proverbs 2:1-22

¹ My son, if thou wilt receive my words, and hide my commandments with thee;
² So that thou incline thine ear unto wisdom, and apply thine heart to understanding;
³ Yea, if thou criest after knowledge, and liftest up thy voice for understanding;

⁴ If thou seekest her as silver, and searchest for her as for hid treasures;

⁵ Then shalt thou understand the fear of the LORD, and find the knowledge of God.

⁶ For the LORD giveth wisdom: out of his mouth cometh knowledge and understanding.

⁷ He layeth up sound wisdom for the righteous: he is a buckler to them that walk uprightly.

⁸ He keepeth the paths of judgment, and preserveth the way of his saints.

⁹ Then shalt thou understand righteousness, and judgment, and equity; yea, every good path.

¹⁰ When wisdom entereth into thine heart, and knowledge is pleasant unto thy soul;

¹¹ Discretion shall preserve thee, understanding shall keep thee:

¹² To deliver thee from the way of the evil man, from the man that speaketh froward things;

¹³ Who leave the paths of uprightness, to walk in the ways of darkness;

¹⁴ Who rejoice to do evil, and delight in the frowardness of the wicked;

¹⁵ Whose ways are crooked, and they froward in their paths:

¹⁶ To deliver thee from the strange woman, even from the stranger which flattereth with her words;

¹⁷ Which forsaketh the guide of her youth, and forgetteth the covenant of her God.

¹⁸ For her house inclineth unto death, and her paths unto the dead.

¹⁹ *None that go unto her return again, neither take they hold of the paths of life.*

²⁰ *That thou mayest walk in the way of good men, and keep the paths of the righteous.*
²¹ *For the upright shall dwell in the land, and the perfect shall remain in it.*
²² *But the wicked shall be cut off from the earth, and the transgressors shall be rooted out of it.*

Proverbs 3:1-35

¹ *My son, forget not my law; but let thine heart keep my commandments:*
² *For length of days, and long life, and peace, shall they add to thee.*
³ *Let not mercy and truth forsake thee: bind them about thy neck; write them upon the table of thine heart:*
⁴ *So shalt thou find favour and good understanding in the sight of God and man.*
⁵ *Trust in the LORD with all thine heart; and lean not unto thine own understanding.*
⁶ *In all thy ways acknowledge him, and he shall direct thy paths.*
⁷ *Be not wise in thine own eyes: fear the LORD, and depart from evil.*
⁸ *It shall be health to thy navel, and marrow to thy bones.*
⁹ *Honour the LORD with thy substance, and with the firstfruits of all thine increase:*

¹⁰ So shall thy barns be filled with plenty, and thy presses shall burst out with new wine.
¹¹ My son, despise not the chastening of the LORD; neither be weary of his correction:
¹² For whom the LORD loveth he correcteth; even as a father the son in whom he delighteth. ¹³ Happy is the man that findeth wisdom, and the man that getteth understanding.
¹⁴ For the merchandise of it is better than the merchandise of silver, and the gain thereof than fine gold.
¹⁵ She is more precious than rubies: and all the things thou canst desire are not to be compared unto her.
¹⁶ Length of days is in her right hand; and in her left hand riches and honour.
¹⁷ Her ways are ways of pleasantness, and all her paths are peace.
¹⁸ She is a tree of life to them that lay hold upon her: and happy is every one that retaineth her. ¹⁹ The LORD by wisdom hath founded the earth; by understanding hath he established the heavens.
²⁰ By his knowledge the depths are broken up, and the clouds drop down the dew.
²¹ My son, let not them depart from thine eyes: keep sound wisdom and discretion:
²² So shall they be life unto thy soul, and grace to thy neck.
²³ Then shalt thou walk in thy way safely, and thy foot shall not stumble.

²⁴ When thou liest down, thou shalt not be afraid: yea, thou shalt lie down, and thy sleep shall be sweet.
²⁵ Be not afraid of sudden fear, neither of the desolation of the wicked, when it cometh.
²⁶ For the LORD shall be thy confidence, and shall keep thy foot from being taken.
²⁷ Withhold not good from them to whom it is due, when it is in the power of thine hand to do it.
²⁸ Say not unto thy neighbour, Go, and come again, and to morrow I will give; when thou hast it by thee.
²⁹ Devise not evil against thy neighbour, seeing he dwelleth securely by thee.
³⁰ Strive not with a man without cause, if he have done thee no harm.
³¹ Envy thou not the oppressor, and choose none of his ways.
³² For the froward is abomination to the LORD: but his secret is with the righteous.
³³ The curse of the LORD is in the house of the wicked: but he blesseth the habitation of the just. ³⁴ Surely he scorneth the scorners: but he giveth grace unto the lowly.
³⁵ The wise shall inherit glory: but shame shall be the promotion of fools.

As you read the scriptures above it becomes clear who represents the HOLY GHOST, and Wisdom. We are given a clear description of the Holy Ghost's characterization and the spiritual functions under Her care. Both blessings and curses are outlined, resulting from our acceptance or rejection of the lesson presented. Amen.

Tree of Life

The Tree of Life is one of the most mysterious subjects within Christianity. It is only mentioned 10 times within the scriptures of the Bible, yet it involves lifesaving information for the entire world! Have you ever wondered who or what the Tree of Life is? Meditate upon the following scripture references as you seek the truth!

> *And unto man he said, Behold, the fear of the Lord, that is wisdom; and to depart from evil is understanding. ~ Job 28:28*

> *She is a tree of life to them that lay hold upon her: and happy is every one that retaineth her. ~ Proverbs 3:18*

> *The fear of the LORD is the beginning of wisdom: a good understanding have all they*

that do his commandments: his praise endureth for ever. ~ *Psalms 111:10*

And out of the ground made the LORD God to grow every tree that is pleasant to the sight, and good for food; the tree of life also in the midst of the garden, and the tree of knowledge of good and evil. ~ *Genesis 2:9*

And the LORD God said, Behold, the man is become as one of us, to know good and evil: and now, lest he put forth his hand, and take also of the tree of life, and eat, and live for ever: ~ *Genesis 3:22*

Therefore the LORD God sent him forth from the garden of Eden, to till the ground from whence he was taken. ~ *Genesis 3:23*

So he drove out the man; and he placed at the east of the garden of Eden Cherubims, and a flaming sword which turned every way, to keep the way of the tree of life. ~ *Genesis 3:24*

The fruit of the righteous is a tree of life; and he that winneth souls is wise. ~ *Proverbs 11:30*

Hope deferred maketh the heart sick, but when the desire cometh, it is a tree of life. ~ *Proverbs 13:12*

A wholesome tongue is a tree of life, but perverseness therein is a breach in the spirit.
~ Proverbs 15:4

He that hath an ear, let him hear what the Spirit saith unto the churches; To him that overcometh will I give to eat of the tree of life, which is in the midst of the paradise of God.
~ Revelation 2:7

In the midst of the street of it, and on either side of the river, was there the tree of life, which bare twelve manner of fruits, and yielded her fruit every month: and the leaves of the tree were for the healing of the nations.
~ Revelation 22:2[5]

Blessed are they that do his commandments, that they may have right to the tree of life and may enter in through the gates into the city. ~ Revelation 22:14

On earth, Lucifer immediately began a plot to get even with God, thus his plot to deceive Adam and Eve. Lucifer knew the unspoken and profound existence and love between Eve and the Holy Ghost. He also knew the protectiveness and unspeakable

---

[5] This biblical reference is to the offsprings of the Holy Ghost who is female and The Tree of Life. Woman is the fruit produced that sheds her blood each month through the menstrual process. This process is for the healing and rebuilding of the people on earth. All female humans are connected to God by the Holy Ghost.

love and devotion between the LORD and the Holy Ghost! God has even informed us through holy scriptures that the Holy Ghost is extra special. <u>According to scripture, to blaspheme or ridicule the Holy Ghost is an unforgivable sin.</u>

> *And whosoever speaketh a word against the Son of man, it shall be forgiven him: but whosoever speaketh against the Holy Ghost, it shall not be forgiven him, neither in this world, neither in the world to come. ~ Matthew 12:32*

Many have contemplated why this is so and offered beliefs that do not correctly address the answer. Based on this revelation, now we know, thus saith the LORD God! The Holy Ghost **Is** the Spiritual Counterpart of "Elohim," which consists of two parts known as Adonai and El Shaddai!

Again, mankind trying to "play" God has justified the plurality of "Elohim" as not really being plural. Some claim this while stating that the word in Hebrew is singular. All of this might seem like chaos, but it confirms that God's revelation is true! Remember, men and not God wrote the Bible! Yes, I do believe God inspired the holy scriptures, but it does not ever replace the divine voice of the LORD! Just look at Paul as an example. He was an Old Testament bible scholar and believed all that was written. Yet, he persecuted the men and women who spoke of the teachings and scholarship of Jesus Christ only because he believed that they contradicted the teachings in the Law or what we know as the Old Testament. Those speaking for Jesus Christ our Lord expressed the words received directly from Him! Such is the case with my revelations. I know nothing except what the LORD God Almighty teaches me, and I will forever stand upon the truths of these teachings!

Be assured that I am not trying to alter anyone's preconceived conviction or convince anyone of the authenticity of the teachings I received from God. Still, I am also committed to NOT be swayed to abandon or walk away from what has been given to me! It is truly my prayer that ALL can enter the presence of God and smell the sweet savor of His breath while resting in His presence! I invite you all to come at the request of the LORD, but I cannot depart!

~ 15 ~

STOP BLAMING EVE

The whole world holds Eve accountable for the sinfulness and disobedience that plague Planet Earth….STOP blaming her! The plan with the serpent was carried out just as God designed it to be. If you believe God truly is God Almighty, do you not know He knew what would happen? Could God not have known what the serpent was up to when he approached Eve? Could the LORD not have changed it all? There would be no change as it happened perfectly as He planned, so STOP blaming Eve for sin entering the world as she followed the Master Plan of God!

According to the LORD, Adam was given more of the LORD's strategic plan than Eve. The LORD knew what the serpent (AKA: Lucifer/Satan) was up to and the devious, cunning nature he has. The Bible makes it plain that the serpent is identical to Satan and the devil!

> *And the great dragon was cast out, that old serpent, called the Devil, and Satan, which deceiveth the whole world: he was cast out into the earth, and his angels were cast out with him. ~ Revelation 12:9*

Adam was given the charge to stay by the side of Eve and watch over her always! Wherever she was to go, so was he. Adam was never to leave Eve unprotected. Therefore, when Eve asked Adam to eat the fruit from the forbidden tree, as she had already done, he was presented with a difficult decision. He knew that if he did not eat the forbidden fruit, Eve would be put out of the garden alone, which would cause him to leave her unprotected in violation of God's instructions to him. What an agonizing and challenging reality he faced! Yet, he was assured that God alone knew and understood his level of pain. He had to eat the fruit to be always in her presence as her unwavering protector assigned by God Almighty! So, STOP blaming Eve!

The strategic plan set in motion by God was masterful, creating the foundation for the birth of Jesus that could not be imagined by the serpent or stopped at any point. Eve, a woman, was instrumental to the success of God's plan. God cursed the serpent for the attempted harm designed to separate Him from Eve. God, being truly God, was aware of the serpent's evil motive!

When God declared that the serpent and woman would be enemies forever, it was also part of His Master Plan. God wanted the world to know that He would take what appeared to be the weaker species of His creation and destroy all works of evil! Yes, women. That means you and me! The weaker we are, the stronger God is. You see, nothing can interfere with or change the plans of God, not even the acts of evil.

There is so much that is processed into the Master Plan of God that truly shows that He is God! Evil is no match for God in any way. The family structure of mankind is of great importance to God. It must be done His way. He gave Adam the starring role to set His plan in motion, with Eve as his costar. All Adam had to do was obey God and follow His instructions. Eve, as the companion and help mate of Adam, was to be forever the loyal and kind creature that she was made to be. Through her, the Spirit and Strength of God flows into the earthly family structure when following His plan. Adam, the man, was chosen as the "caretaker and protector" of the family, a role he is destined to fulfill today. Man plays this role as he is the strongest and wisest of all creatures. However, these characteristics are God-given and cannot be mastered alone. See the perfect Godly family structure below:

God's Order of the Family

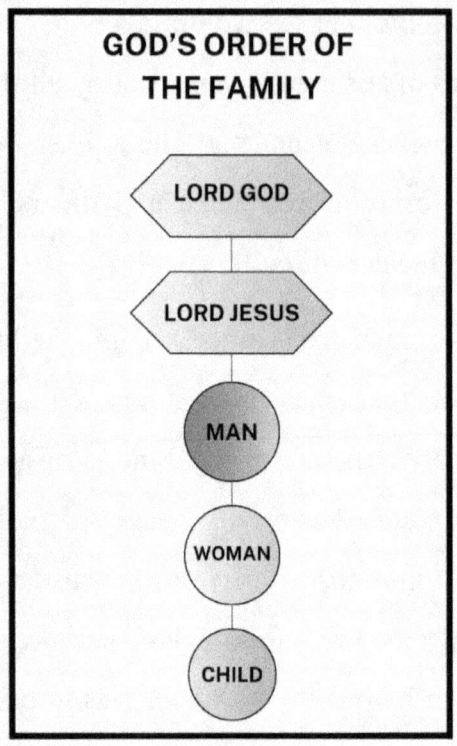

The LORD God Almighty is the Master of all creation. Jesus Christ is the only living Son of God, but is also God, and the Head of man. Jesus is devoted to the security and completion of the family structure that is outlined above. This structure is in place to give the needed love and protection for the woman and child.

Satan's Re-Ordering of the Family *(Phase 1)*

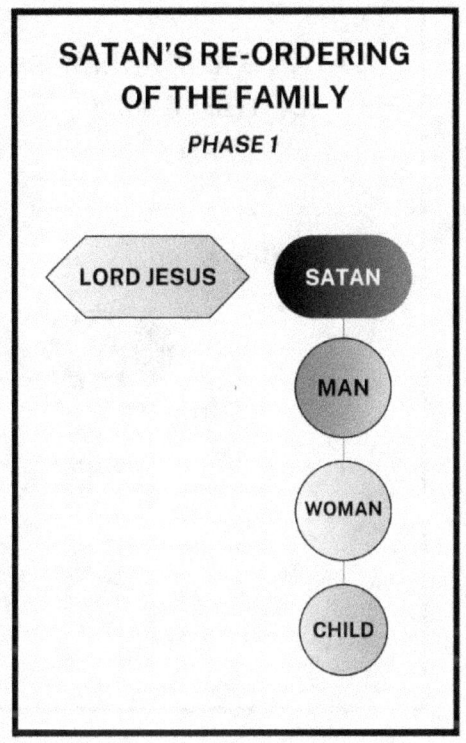

Jesus pleads with man to trust Him and follow His lead. He assures man that he is filled with the Wisdom of God that will replenish his soul continually. Satan continues to cause man to go astray by showing him multiple ways to destroy the woman and child. When man rebels, Jesus moves and accepts his will.

Satan's Re-Ordering of the Family *(Phase 2)*

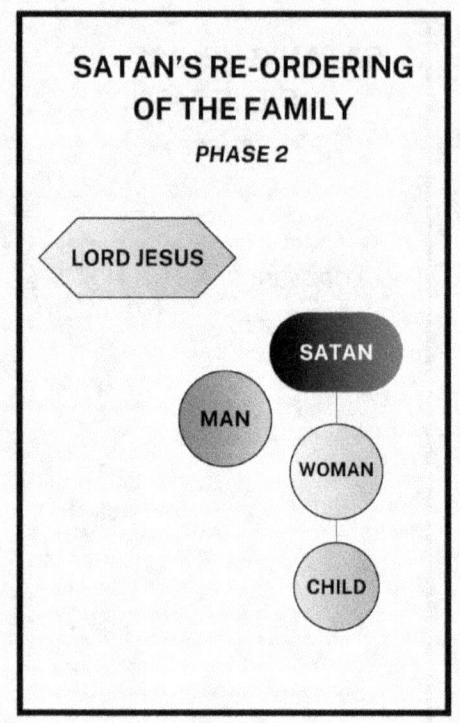

Satan works on destroying the woman who is beloved of God. She is the offspring of the HOLY GHOST. Man is given great riches and fame so he can denounce God. The woman is convinced that she does not need God. Without the man as her head or God as her Savior, she is helpless to defend herself and ultimately leaves her child to be guided by the enemy of the LORD. She is then removed.

Satan's Re-Ordering of the Family *(Phase 3)*

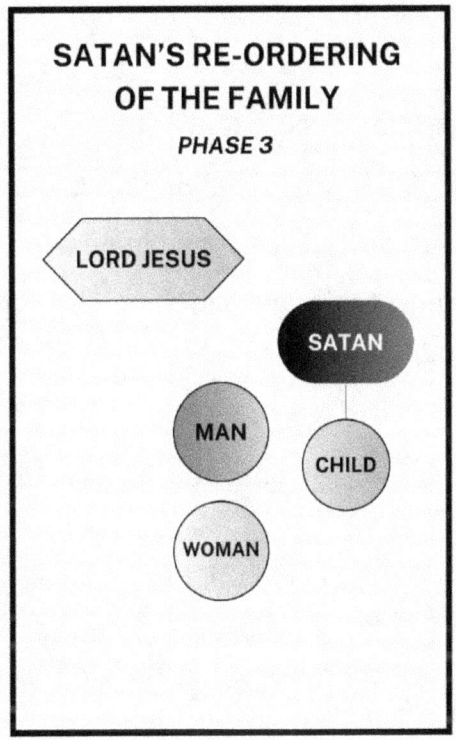

The ultimate goal has been reached as the child now stands alone and without defenses. Satan was previously destroyed by the blows of woman! A child emerged from the woman who caused him to fall. Woman and child will once again hit Satan with a deadly blow. Since Satan does not know how or when this will occur, he works endlessly to destroy women and children.

> *But I want you to understand that the head of every man is Christ, the head of a wife is her husband, and the head of Christ is God.*
> *~ 1 Corinthians 11:3 (ESV)*

Above all things, the Family structure is the strength and power of the LORD God Almighty! We know and honor Him through our surrendered hearts and minds. He searches the heart of mankind for the truths and beliefs held within. The scripture in Psalms 139 declares:

Psalm 139:23-24

> *[23] Search me, O God, and know my heart: try me, and know my thoughts:*
> *[24] And see if there be any wicked way in me, and lead me in the way everlasting.*

It is here that our LORD either accepts or rejects our praise and worship. The heart does not lie, and God cannot be deceived. Please know that this is the setting where our genuine worshipping relationship with God begins! Please cry out to Him and allow God to search your heart and dissect your soul. Daily, I seek His face and trust Him. He knows my heart, my true intent, and desire to forever be by His side and obey His every will for my life!

James 4:5-10

⁵ Do ye think that the scripture saith in vain, The spirit that dwelleth in us lusteth to envy?

⁶ But he giveth more grace. Wherefore he saith, God resisteth the proud, but giveth grace unto the humble.

⁷ Submit yourselves therefore to God. Resist the devil, and he will flee from you.

⁸ Draw nigh to God, and he will draw nigh to you. Cleanse your hands, ye sinners; and purify your hearts, ye double minded.

⁹ Be afflicted, and mourn, and weep: let your laughter be turned to mourning, and your joy to heaviness.

¹⁰ Humble yourselves in the sight of the Lord, and he shall lift you up.

Once the LORD knows we are genuinely willing to surrender our total heart, soul, mind, and body to Him, He presents us as a gift to the Lord Jesus Christ. Jesus is instructed to train and prepare us for living for Him and walking in His Perfect Will! We are placed in a bubble of protection that we cannot see or understand.

The LORD God then remains silent as Jesus carries out His Master Plan.

As I walked with Jesus and received His daily guidance, my world turned upside down! Nothing I knew before was available to me, and the world as I knew it was gone! There was no one to turn to for advice or conversation. I did not understand the degree of pain and suffering endured. With every cry came more intense problems and suffering! I found myself reaching out to others, which only increased my pain. When all paths had been exhausted, and I was forced to come face to face with the understanding that there would be no rescue outside of God, I ceased to fight and ceased to be! I was no longer representing "me" but came to rest in the arms of the LORD! All pain vanished while in His arms, and what had once seemed to be insurmountable problems that could not be overcome were irrelevant and insignificant. Jesus was searching out my heart and cleaning out the debris from within, which was the source of my pain and suffering. He was Dissecting My Soul!

One of the most essential things I learned was the blessing of being called ***"Woman."*** I discovered I should never fear being known as the least among "men." Eve (woman) was not created from the dust of the ground but was **made and molded** by the very hands of God by using a rib taken from Adam.[6] She was made to be a powerful instrument of His love! The woman was made to always rely upon Him and pass on this intimacy and blessing to mankind. Therefore, it should always be the role of "women" to endure the hardships of life so that others can survive!

Jesus, upon completing the dissection of the heart of "woman," began the process of perfecting His Perfect Will for "Adam" (Man). Eve was first in this process since God knew Satan would seek her out as the weakest and most vulnerable link to continue his plot against the LORD. Also, Adam would have greater difficulty in following God's Master Plan. Adam's path was difficult, not because he was weak, but rather due to the complicated instructions and requirements he was given! It took Adam more time to understand God's mission. Once he understood, he became the master warrior that God needed. He knew and understood his role, carrying it out perfectly even when others couldn't. It is most often the strategy of the Lord God to

---

[6] Genesis 2:22: And the rib, which the LORD God had taken from man, made he a woman, and brought her unto the man.

give His disciples or followers tasks that defy the normal intellectual understanding of man. He expects His followers to go forward even in the face of a lack of knowledge.

Biblical scriptures inform us of the great intellect of Adam and how it was used in his relationship with the LORD. Knowing this, can you imagine his thoughts as he worked through his dilemma? <u>He was so in love with the LORD</u>. He did not want to depart from the great garden in which he lived and not bask daily within God's presence, but it was more important that he obey the perfect will of the LORD than entertain his desires. He then knew he had to "eat" the fruit as Eve had, so he could remain by her side as the great protector assigned to him by God, even though it would require him to leave the garden along with Eve! He trusted God above all the thoughts that entered his mind!

Once man was charged with the spiritual and physical well-being of woman, Satan attempted to become more active in their lives. As God whispered His revelations into the ears of the woman, she was instructed to teach them to her husband to keep Satan from directly attacking her.

Ephesians 5:28-33

²⁸ So ought men to love their wives as their own bodies. He that loveth his wife loveth himself.

²⁹ For no man ever yet hated his own flesh; but nourisheth and cherisheth it, even as the Lord the church:

³⁰ For we are members of his body, of his flesh, and of his bones.

³¹ For this cause shall a man leave his father and mother, and shall be joined unto his wife, and they two shall be one flesh.

³² This is a great mystery, but I speak concerning Christ and the church.

³³ Nevertheless let every one of you in particular so love his wife even as himself; and the wife see that she reverence her husband.

The scriptures even tell us that this is a great mystery! Yet, it is one that mankind, via the guidance of Satan, uses to cause further attacks upon Woman!

~ 16 ~

Suicide is Encouraged & Assisted by Satan

An additional mystery God provided relates to Satan's desire to kill off the human creation of God. Therefore, suicide is a method used to accomplish this evil goal. Suicide is simply one dying by one's own hand as directed by evil forces. Everyone will die at some point, but why would anyone prematurely die at their own will? Is it truly their choice to do so? Most people list this as resulting from depression or disillusionment with life! I, however, attribute it all to the acts of evil forces as the LORD has taught me! Historically, my view was believed to be the truth until the Greek Physician Hippocrates[7] set forth an understanding that mental illness was **not** spiritually or demonically related to mental health but rather is a physiological issue instead. This, too, was an evil lie that has been believed to

---

[7] American Experience, PBS. (2018, June 29). Treatments for mental Illness. *American Experience | PBS.* https://www.pbs.org/wgbh/americanexperience/features/nash-treatments-mental-illness/

this day! Imagine the lives saved and the gains had the original truth of this issue remained!

Let's first examine the area of "depression" or "mental illness" as God Himself has taught me. Let's consider the mind of mankind, which the LORD created. Please keep going with me until the end of this book! You owe it to yourself to hear what God is saying to us all and then pray about what you believe. If you honestly seek an explanation, God has assured me that He will respond even if you do not know Him.

Know that man is not a thinking being! Instead, he is created and made to take the thoughts presented to him and present these thoughts to God for understanding.

Corinthians 10:3-5

> *³ For though we walk in the flesh, we do not war after the flesh:*
> *⁴ (For the weapons of our warfare are not carnal, but mighty through God to the pulling down of strong holds;),*
> *⁵ Casting down imaginations, and every high thing that exalteth itself against the knowledge of God, and bringing into captivity every thought to the obedience of Christ;*

According to Almighty God, all thoughts received in the mind of man are either from Him or Satan. The referenced scripture from 2 Corinthians tells us that we are warring with the devil with EVERY thought we entertain. The devil wants us to believe we are smart and intelligent and do not need to rely upon anyone but ourselves. He boosts our egos and makes us self-reliant. However, God is instructing us to take captive EVERY thought that enters our mind and bring it obediently unto Him. Here, our LORD removes all evil thoughts from us, battles the devil, and instructs us further!

Our job is to take each thought that enters our mind and pray to God for truth. This lesson was one of the first things that the LORD taught me. Hearing and believing this mystery from God has strengthened my faith and increased my love relationship with Father God, the Great I AM! It has allowed me to measure all thoughts against the teachings of my LORD and correctly discern His will for me in all matters!

The problem is that we all want to possess unspeakable knowledge and believe we are wise in most issues of our lives. Again, God taught me it is better to know nothing at all in this world than to live defenselessly pretending to know. All that is needed is to "truly know and trust Him!"

Satan convinces depressed people that life would be better if they were dead. He says their pain will be gone, and they will be at peace. What a lie this is! Suicide sends us straight to hell, thus saith the LORD! A terrible darkness presents itself to those who are depressed or saddened. Many reach this phase through drugs, alcohol, sexual sin, or through generational curses, to name a few. God has shown me that individuals assigned to mental institutions are demon-possessed! Realizing the controversy of this statement, I ask you to remember I am not commanded to appease anyone but to explain honestly and truthfully what God has said or revealed. Here I invite those who have a true relationship with Father God to ask Him to give you an ear to hear what thus saith the LORD!

I've noticed that God often asks questions before providing explanations. As we discussed the issues of suicide, I could not grasp the need for anyone to kill themselves or willingly follow evil. Rather than trying to explain how this could be, I found myself in a very dark place. The darkness was so horrible that words cannot explain. At the time, I had just undergone back surgery and was in a lot of pain. The medicines prescribed by my surgeon were powerful, and I often felt that I was not in control of my body or mind. It appeared that reality was quite elusive! One of my students flew in from Illinois to CA to care for me. I recall believing she was working against me, and I told her so! I soon realized that it was all in my mind and not actually occurring. This was a trick from the enemy, courtesy of the intoxicating medicine prescribed!

During this period, I was enveloped in profound darkness, and I struggled to comprehend what was happening to me. I do recall that the thoughts in my mind urged me to escape the darkness by leaping down a cliff with bright lights below. I looked around but didn't see God. As I purposed to follow this thought, the LORD grabbed me and revealed Himself! He wanted to know what I was doing, and I explained I was looking for Him as the pain was unbearable and that the darkness was too overwhelming! He held me close and reminded me of the promise He had made me. He promised that He would never leave me alone! Even though I might not see Him, I always had to trust that He was there. He left me again amid great darkness that was worse than before! This time, I found myself amid a field of serpents of all kinds. I had nowhere to walk or step as they were everywhere. Although I cried, I walked through until the way was clear and the darkness had disappeared. Although my heart was frantic, I was trusting everything would be alright, just as God had promised. One of my students was with me as I walked through the bed of serpents, and neither of us was harmed. God appeared again and rescued us!

He was testing my understanding and faith to know that he would always be with me, no matter the danger, if my love for Him was real! I started to imagine how one would feel in this situation without the help of the LORD while listening to the thoughts and lies of Satan! God knows our stresses, so He desperately tries to get all souls to walk in His light. It was through these experiences with darkness that Jesus allowed me to understand suicide and how it is possible. Again, the tricks by Satan can NEVER prevail when Jesus abides in the heart!

Parents and caretakers have a great responsibility here. All children are born with an innate sense of the spiritual world and, more importantly, a clear understanding of who God is. However, this spiritual knowledge must be nourished and encouraged daily. Satan is constantly leading our children on an alternate path to the reality of Jesus Christ. I know this to be true, as God has had me take young children into my home to keep them safe from spiritual danger while teaching me how this was happening. I will not go into detail here, as that is an entirely different subject. Just know that Satan appears with gifts of all kinds and contradicts the teachings of the parents and the LORD! When children attempt to tell their parents about such visits, they do not believe them. Therefore, if the parent is lost, so will the child be unless God intervenes. Listen to your children and prioritize their needs and desires above all else in your life. Let them know they can always count on you. Never place anything, not even your work, before your child's needs! When this happens, Satan instead gives them the attention they desire. If you are on a phone call and your child needs your attention, ask the person on the line to hold for a moment while you respond to your child's needs. This action helps them to know they are more important to you than anyone else. Isn't this what we expect God to do when we cry out to Him?

Many people, and mainly our children, are suffering daily at the hands of Satan with inflicted medical and personality issues that stem from demonic possession! Help them as you expect the LORD to help you. Amen.

~ 17 ~

Helpless in the Hands of God

The LORD expects total submission to His perfect will as we follow Him! If we use Jesus Christ as our example, we must follow His lead. The scriptures demonstrate that He submitted Himself unto the LORD before warring with the devil. Jesus Christ was baptized by John the Baptist and immediately spent the next 40 days and nights in prayer and fasting as He humbled Himself to His Father! This action spiritually prepared Him to resist the devil and follow the perfect will of God!

> *Submit yourselves therefore to God. Resist the devil, and he will flee from you. ~ James 4:7*

This scripture clarifies that we MUST first repent and then submit ourselves to God BEFORE engaging in warfare with the devil! I have witnessed many who claim not to need to repent or humble themselves to God yet claim they have proper standing with God to battle Satan! This will never work! Jesus Himself followed this exact path to have success over the devil! This was simply a way of teaching mankind what must be done to be successful.

Here, we will encounter the wiles of the devil more than ever as he showers us with praise to encourage us to stand alone without God. This is not new as he tried the same thing with Jesus: he tempted Him to take control of Himself after Jesus had fasted 40 days and nights. Satan first determined what he thought the Lord wanted most at that time…food! While knowing that He was truly God, Satan still bargained with the Lord by offering Him food in exchange for worshiping him. Remember that even though things sound good, they might not be the will of God. Faithful followers of the Lord abandon what is best for themselves and focus only on what thus saith the LORD God! This is what it means to be helpless in the hands of the LORD. There is no thought given to personal needs, but rather how we can respond to and follow the will of the LORD.

If we are to become True Christians, we must always be dependent on God. He sees all and knows all. He cannot be deceived by evil. Due to who He is, we can always trust His leadership. To depart from God is to be in rebellion against His will! Helplessness is not a weakness, as viewed by many. It utilizes the strength of the LORD instead of relying on our own understanding of what we think should be done. The adversary of God orchestrates such thoughts and imaginations.

I've learned to be helpless before the LORD as He teaches me how to live. Every job or primary task I have ever had since truly falling in love with the LORD God has been directed by Him. My job performance most often exceeded that of others, and my superiors always recognized my success. He always proved Himself to me without the need to do so. There is no one that I would rather follow than the LORD!

Section III

Further Lessons Learned While Resting in the Presence of God

~ 18 ~

Living a Life of Job

At the beginning of our relationship, I asked the LORD to teach me everything He knew. After a considerable amount of time, He told me to read the book of Job and come back later. At the time, I did not know very much about Job. I did as He asked and was horrified that my LORD had encouraged Satan to attack Job!

After reading as I had been instructed, God responded by asking me a series of questions, as He often does. By the end of that conversation, I realized it was love and pride that had prompted God to promote the strengths of Job. The LORD allowed me to know that when we want Him, All of Him, we would be granted the right to hear and see things that others could not. Our growth and understanding are revealed by what we do with the knowledge gained.

Job was given much due to his trust, faith, and love of God. Yet, knowing Job's every thought, the LORD knew there was much more for him to learn. Rather than trying to convince Job of his faults, it was better that he be allowed to experience them and seal his understanding.

Job 3:25-26

²⁵ For the thing which I greatly feared is come upon me, and that which I was afraid of is come unto me.
²⁶ I was not in safety, neither had I rest, neither was I quiet; yet trouble came.

Due to the degree of teaching and training given to Job, God truly desired him to fight harder against His enemy than he did but knew that he would not! There was another conversation between God and Job that supports my statements. God reminded Job He alone was God, and whatever he thought he knew was not enough to manage his life alone!

Job 38:1-41

¹ Then the LORD answered Job out of the whirlwind, and said,
² Who is this that darkeneth counsel by words without knowledge?
³ Gird up now thy loins like a man; for I will demand of thee, and answer thou me.

4 Where wast thou when I laid the foundations of the earth? declare, if thou hast understanding.
5 Who hath laid the measures thereof, if thou knowest? or who hath stretched the line upon it?
6 Whereupon are the foundations thereof fastened? or who laid the corner stone thereof; 7 When the morning stars sang together, and all the sons of God shouted for joy?
8 Or who shut up the sea with doors, when it brake forth, as if it had issued out of the womb?
9 When I made the cloud the garment thereof, and thick darkness a swaddling band for it,
10 And brake up for it my decreed place, and set bars and doors,
11 And said, Hitherto shalt thou come, but no further: and here shall thy proud waves be stayed?
12 Hast thou commanded the morning since thy days; and caused the dayspring to know his place;
13 That it might take hold of the ends of the earth, that the wicked might be shaken out of it?
14 It is turned as clay to the seal; and they stand as a garment.
15 And from the wicked their light is withholden, and the high arm shall be broken.
16 Hast thou entered into the springs of the sea? or hast thou walked in the search of the depth?

17 Have the gates of death been opened unto thee? or hast thou seen the doors of the shadow of death?

18 Hast thou perceived the breadth of the earth? declare if thou knowest it all.

19 Where is the way where light dwelleth? and as for darkness, where is the place thereof,

20 That thou shouldest take it to the bound thereof, and that thou shouldest know the paths to the house thereof?

21 Knowest thou it, because thou wast then born? or because the number of thy days is great?

22 Hast thou entered into the treasures of the snow? or hast thou seen the treasures of the hail,

23 Which I have reserved against the time of trouble, against the day of battle and war?

24 By what way is the light parted, which scattereth the east wind upon the earth?

25 Who hath divided a watercourse for the overflowing of waters, or a way for the lightning of thunder;

26 To cause it to rain on the earth, where no man is; on the wilderness, wherein there is no man; 27 To satisfy the desolate and waste ground; and to cause the bud of the tender herb to spring forth?

28 Hath the rain a father? or who hath begotten the drops of dew?

29 Out of whose womb came the ice? and the hoary frost of heaven, who hath gendered it?

³⁰ The waters are hid as with a stone, and the face of the deep is frozen.
³¹ Canst thou bind the sweet influences of Pleiades, or loose the bands of Orion?
³² Canst thou bring forth Mazzaroth in his season? or canst thou guide Arcturus with his sons?
³³ Knowest thou the ordinances of heaven? canst thou set the dominion thereof in the earth?
³⁴ Canst thou lift up thy voice to the clouds, that abundance of waters may cover thee?
³⁵ Canst thou send lightnings, that they may go, and say unto thee, Here we are?
³⁶ Who hath put wisdom in the inward parts? or who hath given understanding to the heart?
³⁷ Who can number the clouds in wisdom? or who can stay the bottles of heaven,
³⁸ When the dust groweth into hardness, and the clods cleave fast together?
³⁹ Wilt thou hunt the prey for the lion? or fill the appetite of the young lions,
⁴⁰ When they couch in their dens, and abide in the covert to lie in wait?
⁴¹ Who provideth for the raven his food? when his young ones cry unto God, they wander for lack of meat.

Job 40:1-24

¹ Moreover the LORD answered Job, and said,

2 Shall he that contendeth with the Almighty instruct him? he that reproveth God, let him answer it.
3 Then Job answered the LORD, and said,
4 Behold, I am vile; what shall I answer thee? I will lay mine hand upon my mouth.
5 Once have I spoken; but I will not answer: yea, twice; but I will proceed no further.
6 Then answered the LORD unto Job out of the whirlwind, and said,
7 Gird up thy loins now like a man: I will demand of thee, and declare thou unto me.
8 Wilt thou also disannul my judgment? wilt thou condemn me, that thou mayest be righteous?
9 Hast thou an arm like God? or canst thou thunder with a voice like him?
10 Deck thyself now with majesty and excellency; and array thyself with glory and beauty.
11 Cast abroad the rage of thy wrath: and behold every one that is proud, and abase him.
12 Look on every one that is proud, and bring him low; and tread down the wicked in their place. 13 Hide them in the dust together; and bind their faces in secret.
14 Then will I also confess unto thee that thine own right hand can save thee.
15 Behold now behemoth, which I made with thee; he eateth grass as an ox.
16 Lo now, his strength is in his loins, and his force is in the navel of his belly.
17 He moveth his tail like a cedar: the sinews of his stones are wrapped together.

18 His bones are as strong pieces of brass; his bones are like bars of iron.
19 He is the chief of the ways of God: he that made him can make his sword to approach unto him.
20 Surely the mountains bring him forth food, where all the beasts of the field play.
21 He lieth under the shady trees, in the covert of the reed, and fens.
22 The shady trees cover him with their shadow; the willows of the brook compass him about.
23 Behold, he drinketh up a river, and hasteth not: he trusteth that he can draw up Jordan into his mouth.
24 He taketh it with his eyes: his nose pierceth through snares. Canst thou draw out leviathan with an hook? or his tongue with a cord which thou lettest down?

Job 41:2-34

2 Canst thou put an hook into his nose? or bore his jaw through with a thorn?
3 Will he make many supplications unto thee? will he speak soft words unto thee?
4 Will he make a covenant with thee? wilt thou take him for a servant for ever?
5 Wilt thou play with him as with a bird? or wilt thou bind him for thy maidens?
6 Shall the companions make a banquet of him? shall they part him among the merchants?

⁷ Canst thou fill his skin with barbed irons? or his head with fish spears?
⁸ Lay thine hand upon him, remember the battle, do no more.
⁹ Behold, the hope of him is in vain: shall not one be cast down even at the sight of him?
¹⁰ None is so fierce that dare stir him up: who then is able to stand before me?
¹¹ Who hath prevented me, that I should repay him? whatsoever is under the whole heaven is mine.
¹² I will not conceal his parts, nor his power, nor his comely proportion.

¹³ Who can discover the face of his garment? or who can come to him with his double bridle?
¹⁴ Who can open the doors of his face? his teeth are terrible round about.
¹⁵ His scales are his pride, shut up together as with a close seal.
¹⁶ One is so near to another, that no air can come between them.
¹⁷ They are joined one to another, they stick together, that they cannot be sundered.
¹⁸ By his neesings a light doth shine, and his eyes are like the eyelids of the morning.
¹⁹ Out of his mouth go burning lamps, and sparks of fire leap out.
²⁰ Out of his nostrils goeth smoke, as out of a seething pot or caldron.
²¹ His breath kindleth coals, and a flame goeth out of his mouth.

²² In his neck remaineth strength, and sorrow is turned into joy before him.
²³ The flakes of his flesh are joined together: they are firm in themselves; they cannot be moved.
²⁴ His heart is as firm as a stone; yea, as hard as a piece of the nether millstone.
²⁵ When he raiseth up himself, the mighty are afraid: by reason of breakings they purify themselves.
²⁶ The sword of him that layeth at him cannot hold: the spear, the dart, nor the habergeon.
²⁷ He esteemeth iron as straw, and brass as rotten wood.
²⁸ The arrow cannot make him flee: slingstones are turned with him into stubble.
²⁹ Darts are counted as stubble: he laugheth at the shaking of a spear.
³⁰ Sharp stones are under him: he spreadeth sharp pointed things upon the mire.
³¹ He maketh the deep to boil like a pot: he maketh the sea like a pot of ointment.
³² He maketh a path to shine after him; one would think the deep to be hoary.
³³ Upon earth there is not his like, who is made without fear.
³⁴ He beholdeth all high things: he is a king over all the children of pride.

Through the previous scriptures from the Book of Job, God has provided further explanations of the meaning of the Sea and the demise that He has presented for its existence. Job knew the power of God and the long-standing trappings of Satan, as illustrated in the description of Behemoth and Leviathan. Yet, he was content to enjoy the intimacy that had developed between him and God. He knew that one day God would call upon him to demonstrate that great love for Him he claimed to possess.

Initially, I could not understand why God was so harsh with Job, but I began to understand as He revealed more of his teachings. You see, God expected Job to resist the wiles of Satan, just as He had been taught to stand against evil, trusting that God would always prevail! He bragged about Job and pointed Satan in his direction as He trusted Job to use the knowledge he had been given! This also allowed God to demonstrate to Job that it is not enough to know the truth, but Job was expected to walk in the belief that he claimed to know! This, too, applies to us today. It does not matter if we, the believers, are seen by others. The LORD expects us to always walk in His revealed truths.

There are so many lessons found within the Book of Job. Many mysteries can validate many of the statements in other portions of this book. I will simply say here that if you believe, or want to know God as He truly is, seek His face fervently, and He will respond. Know He will judge our hearts to see if we are truthfully seeking Him as God. Amen.

~ 19 ~

Trust & Obey

> ⁵ *Trust in the* LORD *with all thine heart; and lean not unto thine own understanding.*
> ⁶ *In all thy ways acknowledge him, and he shall direct thy paths.*
> *~ Proverbs 3:5-6*
>
> *Who is among you that feareth the* LORD, *that obeyeth the voice of his servant, that walketh in darkness, and hath no light? let him trust in the name of the* LORD, *and stay upon his God.*
> *~ Isaiah 50:10*

To KNOW God is to love Him. To love Him is to trust Him. To trust Him is to obey Him. When we obey Him, we follow Him. The most amazing experience any "soul" can have is to know the LORD and know that the soul knows Him. Many claim to know Him but have never experienced the beauty of His presence or experienced His Glory. This is unfortunate as it is available to all. Standing in the presence of the LORD God is greater than anything imaginable and cannot be explained with mere words. Once the Holy Ghost has been introduced to an individual's body, mind, and soul, such a one has indeed changed. When we reach this point and discover truly who God is, there is no room for abandonment of our precious Lord and Savior, Jesus Christ. <u>God has allowed me to understand that experiencing Him in His Glory does not provide an opportunity to leave His presence.</u> If this type of abandonment of the LORD occurs, such a one can NEVER return! To believe otherwise is to allow theology to falsify who God is and to follow demonic teachings not of the LORD God Almighty. It is difficult for some believers to think that they might not have a relationship with God even though they claim to know Him. Maintaining this position is one of the significant wrongs in the Christian life.

Let us analyze the scriptures in Hebrews below that provide the correct biblical perspective on this subject. The scriptures in Hebrews 6:1-6 begin by encouraging those that claim to be believers to leave behind and stop debating old theological concepts that stagnate us. Little is gained in discussions of repentance regarding dead works and having faith in God! These things we should already know if we ARE believers! While living in a surrendered, intimate love relationship with God, there is no need to engage in continued discussions about the doctrines of baptisms, laying on of hands, resurrection of the dead, and eternal judgment. When we KNOW God and love Him with our whole hearts, these things are automatic! Refusing to move beyond this stage highlights the lack of intimacy with the LORD.

Hebrews 6:1-6

> *¹ Therefore leaving the principles of the doctrine of Christ, let us go on unto perfection; not laying again the foundation of repentance from dead works, and of faith toward God,*
> *² Of the doctrine of baptisms, and of laying on of hands, and of resurrection of the dead, and of eternal judgment.*
> *³ And this will we do, if God permit.*
> *⁴ For it is impossible for those who were once enlightened, and have tasted of the heavenly gift, and were made partakers of the Holy Ghost,*
> *⁵ And have tasted the good word of God, and the powers of the world to come,*
> *⁶ If they shall fall away, to renew them again unto repentance; seeing they crucify to themselves the Son of God afresh, and put him to an open shame.*

Even though the scripture is explicitly clear, it is extremely hard for most "Self-Confessing Christians" to receive my words. Many, or perhaps I can biblically state that, three-fourths of all believers, according to the divine revelation of my LORD and supported by the scriptures as recorded in **Mathew:13:18-23, Mark 4: 3-20, and Luke 8:13-18,** have never become true Christian Believers. The heart or "soul" of a man is quickly revealed by the words he speaks or the actions he takes. The LORD evaluates our "surrendered" hearts to Him based on these words or actions.

"Once Saved, Always Saved" Doctrine:

Another critical fact overlooked or improperly taught by today's Christian is that we are Saved if we have uttered the words with our lips. We all assume that because we have confessed to the LORD with our mouths, we have also believed in our hearts. This is not true and is literally crippling the church today! The people are being led to think "true repentance" is unnecessary if the words have been spoken. The LORD God Himself has stated that this is not true!

The added danger in this type of teaching is that "would-be" Christians are led to believe that since they have already confessed with their mouth, they can live any way and be forgiven for all their sins. They are taught the LORD will forgive them for all things by grace. Yes, the LORD will forgive our sins through grace, but there must be true repentance. This faulty belief is based on the "once saved, always saved" doctrine. This controversial doctrine creates a great divide within the body of Christ based on a lack of understanding of what the scriptures teach. The spiritual implications of the wrong understanding of this doctrine can cause absolute damnation to the soul. My "go-to" solution, as taught by the LORD, is to **Trust and Obey** what God is saying. Do not rationalize your actions. What did He say or do? What has God already said about the matter? His ways do not change. We must trust what He has already said. We must obey what He has already charged us to do! We will not go wrong if we utilize these principles as everyday tools to guide us in our relationship with Jesus Christ.

When we commit an error, as we all will do, there is a process for ridding ourselves of the ramifications of sin. First, we must repent. <u>We must "TRULY" repent</u>. We must not be guilty of "repeated" same sin activities. God has shown me that when and if we repeat those sins after asking for forgiveness, we never truly repented! If we never truly repented, then we have NOT been forgiven. Many sins are committed repeatedly without true repentance. This allows Satan to mock the body of Christ for its apparent ignorance of the truth.

For this is the love of God, that we keep his commandments: and his commandments are not grievous. ~ 1 John 5:3

If ye keep my commandments, ye shall abide in my love; even as I have kept my Father's commandments, and abide in his love. ~ John 15:10

If ye love me, keep my commandments. ~ John 14:15

Let's look at a personal Life example of false repentance. I once knew a lady that was a profound orator, Evangelist, and Preacher of the Gospel. One night, I was awakened by the LORD around 1:00 AM. I was instructed to call this Preacher and say, "God wants you to know that He loves you so much." I made the call. The Preacher listened and then began to cry. Without any words, she hung up the phone. I was clueless about why God wanted me to make this call or why she abruptly hung up. A few days passed, and she called me to ask if God had said anything else. I said no, he had not. I apologized for calling at the hour that I did, but I also explained that I had no choice. She understood. This message was delivered several times in the same manner over a period of months. Finally, I found I was leaving messages on voicemail, and she refused to answer. Soon after, the LORD revealed to me that this Preacher had become possessed by many demons due to repeated sexual sin! He explained each time He had me call, she was engaged in performing such acts. She always repented, according to God, but she never meant what she said and repeated the process over and over. After many attempts to get her attention to no avail, the LORD gave up. She proved she loved the man and her sin more than the Lord Jesus! My heart broke into pieces. Soon, I was uncomfortable in her presence, and she in mine. I prayed often for her and asked God to help her. One day, she invited me to her home for dinner. I was afraid to go, but the Lord Jesus told me to go. When I arrived, I recognized her as the demonic being living inside her, and not as herself. She told me how she hated me. She said that she knew that I knew her secret. Then suddenly, she was herself and started to cry while embracing me ever so tenderly. We cried and prayed together. She admitted everything to me, and said she was weak and had tried to stop but could not! She said she had always repented and did not understand why God was not there for her. She promised to call me each time she was tempted, and we would stand together. She never called. She never changed and never "truly" repented, saith the LORD God Almighty. She later became engaged to marry this man who was already married during her relationship with him and failed to tell me. God told me and asked me to call her and tell her that it was NOT His will that she do this thing. I made the call and said what I was instructed to say. She cursed me out and hung up the phone. She married the man against the will of God. Shortly after that, he started to cheat on her, and she deeply regretted her choice. She lived a life of misery and eventually got a divorce. I do not know if she ever found her way back to the LORD.

Let us examine the scripture below, considering the example provided. We will see what God has to say about those that have truly received the power of the Holy Ghost. This knowledge and wisdom will truly teach us the Truth of who God is.

> *4 For it is impossible for those who were once enlightened, and have tasted of the heavenly gift, and were made partakers of the Holy Ghost,*
> *5 And have tasted the good word of God, and the powers of the world to come,*
> *6 If they shall fall away, to renew them again unto repentance; seeing they crucify to*

> *themselves the Son of God afresh, and put him to an open shame.*

The scripture above states it is impossible to renew unto repentance such a one that has been enlightened but has ***fallen away***. The key here is "fallen away." This implies that one must first have been a partaker of the power of the Holy Ghost. Such a one must first have been exposed to the presence and true knowledge of the LORD God Almighty. No one can "fall away" without first having been there! I provide here the explanation that my LORD has given me.

1. When we accept Jesus Christ as our Lord and Savior, confessing our faith as such with our mouth, and genuinely believing and accepting Him as Lord in our heart, to have been given the privilege to KNOW the LORD, to see and walk with Jesus Christ as the "LIVING" Son of God, AND to have received the indwelling power of the Holy Ghost, why would anyone EVER walk away? To do so is spiritual suicide. When a soul has tasted or consumed the Word, Jesus Christ Himself as the Son of God, why would He ever be rejected? This "WORD," Jesus Christ, leads us into a path of understanding the spiritual world and all that is

yet to come based on a clear understanding of who God is.

2. When the LORD God Almighty shares all of His wisdom with such a soul, and He is left behind as insufficient, the LORD spews this creature, be it man, woman, or beast, out of His sight forever! There is no way to come back! Repentance is NOT an option! The scripture tells it all. It states it is impossible for such a one to walk away and be forgiven even when he decides to repent or return! Many Christians are being told that they can sin and be forgiven, and this is true. However, this relates only to "true" repentance. True repentance does not allow us to repeat the same mistakes over again. To repeat actions we know are wrong indicates we NEVER truly repented.

3. The scripture in Hebrews does not refer to those who have never known God. Nor is it referring to anyone who has not stood in the actual presence of the LORD God. Unless a soul has stood in the presence of God and has become a partaker of the Holy Ghost, this scripture is not addressed to him! This type of believer has been caught in the web of confusion created by the enemy of God. This confusion is specifically designed to lead us away from God by making us believe we are already living according to the ways of

God. How cunning is the devil that works against the people of God! If we cling to the belief the Holy Ghost is already living within us and we walk away (sin against the LORD) AND that we **can** come back, then the bible is a lie. This is not possible, as the bible is clear on this subject. If we could only grasp this simple concept of understanding who God is vs. the inner workings of the evil that plagues the mind of mankind, it would all be noticeably clear. Satan has blackened the mind and understanding of the concepts and truths of the Holy Scriptures of God. According to the LORD, as documented by scripture, <u>¾ of the Christian world cannot see or find the</u> <u>uncompromising path to the righteousness of God.</u>

~ 20 ~

Testimony After Entering the Presence of the LORD

My original understanding of who God is was damaged by the natural worldview that Satan is still perpetuating. Even in my rejection of Satan with no desire to follow him, God allowed me to see he could still operate as ruler over the thoughts that governed my life. I did not realize I had given him access to my heart using my thoughts! Due to my ignorance, it was in Satan's best interest to allow me to be "good" and continue with goodness rather than try to make me completely unholy or reject God outright. This view would have triggered something within me that would scream a need for change. So, I went through life being an exceptionally good person. In this state of goodness, Satan had planted false views of life itself, distorted my ideas of right and wrong, good and evil, and even allowed me to believe I was a Christian! The "consuming fire" of God battled Satan for me and drew me near to Him. I praise God for being my Savior! He knew that I needed Him when I did not know. He knew the deception that was prevailing in my heart. As I traveled the fiery burning path to reach the presence of the LORD, my eyes saw destruction and evil on every side of me in all forms. The LORD knew that as I walked through the flames in obedience that they would soon appear as cooling waters of truth. I had only to seek His face and listen to His voice to experience His peace. I had to maintain the resolve and will to reach Him at all costs. Through experiencing the love of "I AM," I kept seeking and soon discovered that the flames no longer burned, and there was soothing "living" water that cooled my flesh and restored my soul.

Having lived for 12 to 18 months through what initially seemed like a "living hell," I came out on the other side with a profound knowledge of the reality of the existence of Almighty God. There is no doubt in my mind that Jesus Christ is the living Son of God. I know that I know that the Holy Ghost guides my day and is the Wisdom and Understanding of God Almighty. I had survived God's "consuming fire," experienced His Glory, and lived to talk about it!

After delivering the original message of God to my Illinois church, I was able to rest each night and hoped the life I had previously known would return. This proved not to be the plan of God. The rest period was short-lived. Again, I found myself being instructed by God in every way. God had my full attention since I had not yet returned to work.

I started looking for retail storefronts to open a business. Although I had no skills to be a retailer, I looked anyway with a definite purpose that I did not understand. Within a few months, I found the perfect place in a new shopping plaza remarkably close to my home. As a new plaza, every interior unit had to be completed by the retail owner. I had no money to begin. Yet, I contacted the Plaza Owner and inquired about the space. I informed him I would open a custom clothing store and natural nail salon. I have no idea where this came from since I could not sew and knew nothing about nail care! While preparing for the shop to open, the LORD took control of everything. The little money that I had ran out quickly.

I opened a custom clothing store called TaiVon Fashion Gallery with little to no money. I found a dressmaker who lived nearby, and I took classes to become a Manicurist. Almost immediately, very unusual things began to occur. Since the dressmaker was a self-confessing Christian, I was greatly encouraged. She knew my total reliance upon the LORD God, and all appeared well.

I realized this would not be an ordinary retail store or shop as time passed. Continuously each day, the LORD provided instructions on what to do and how to do them. I had a shop full of valuable sewing equipment I had purchased from a company going out of business. The cost was almost a giveaway. That, too, was orchestrated by the LORD. I went to work each day, not knowing what to expect. I clearly remember the day that changed everything…the day that God THRUST me into the spiritual realm! Now I can see that this is also what happened with Job.

The day started like all the others, except I found myself praying differently before opening the shop for business that day. Once again, the words from my mouth and within my heart were not my own but came from a familiar place that let me know God was about to do something I had no control over. During this prayer, I not only asked the LORD to bind and keep the devil and his hoards away from me and the shop, but if it was His will not to do so, then He would bind him in a particular way that would prevent any evil actions from hurting me, my family, or the shop. I continued to worship God in prayer for what seemed like hours!

Later that morning, when the shop opened for business, my seamstress said we had to get someone to come in and explain how to use the sewing equipment we owned. "The blind hemmer," she said, "will be a great help with alterations." I agreed and promised that I would resolve the problem with the equipment. As we worked in the front of the shop that day, a customer walked in. I was so excited. She was a black lady who wanted to know exactly what we had to offer. She said she was a seamstress. My seamstress asked her if she knew how to use a blind hemmer, and she said yes. I immediately began to pray, asking God to bind my seamstress' words so she would not ask her to go into the back. I looked at the seamstress, and she looked totally confused and upset. I later discovered she was frustrated because she had something to say but could not speak! The customer then moved closer to the clothes in the showcase window and snarled at our use of leather products. She tried to touch the garments as she critiqued them, but she bent over to reach them instead of walking up to them! This was very strange to me and my seamstress. It was as if she was frozen in one spot. Then she walked back to the reception desk where I was and tried to go further into the shop in the back, but again, she was frozen in a spot she could not surpass. Through all this, my spirit cried out to God as I had no idea what was happening but did know that these were not ordinary occurrences.

My prayer that morning was for God to bind the devil in a

special way. However, evil was allowed to enter the shop at the will of God but was restricted to a certain area or spot that could not be crossed. The devil had listened to our spoken desires regarding our need to operate the sewing equipment and attempted to use our needs to get a spiritual hold in a place where he knew he was forbidden to tread. It would have been spiritually disastrous if this woman had been allowed to enter the shop work area! God allowed this evil to come close, knowing that He was there to protect me as I entered spiritual warfare training at His leading.

Through this experience, I was introduced to the true power of prayer and the need to give God total control of my life. I also discovered the power of silence. To have spoken anything at all would have interfered with God's perfect will in an area I had no knowledge or understanding of. The devil was counting on my ignorance to let him in the door. He tried to use that which had been spoken that I and my seamstress expressed as a need. Through this, God also taught me to speak and pray within my heart rather than use words aloud unless I was willing to share those thoughts with the devil. It also let me know everything that comes to us after prayer is not necessarily from the Lord. Satan is always searching for ways to find out what is happening in our hearts and prayers. Be careful when praying aloud! Our open prayers should be to worship and exalt the LORD. All other needs should be silently presented to God within our hearts. Know that all answers to open prayer are not necessarily from the LORD. The most important lesson I learned was to try all spirits by the Spirit of the LORD God Almighty. If there is a contradiction in any way, then I walk away content to be within the perfect will of God.

~ 21 ~

Understanding the Spiritual World

> *But the hour cometh, and now is, when the true worshippers shall worship the Father in spirit and in truth: for the Father seeketh such to worship him. ~ John 4:23*
>
> *God is a Spirit: and they that worship him must worship him in spirit and in truth ~ John 4:24*
>
> *It is the spirit that quickeneth; the flesh profiteth nothing: the words that I speak unto you, they are spirit, and they are life. ~ John 6:63*

We live in a spiritual world, whether we know it or not. The entire universe is spiritual. Spiritual reality is made up of good and bad, or plainly spoken, of God and the devil. One must only accept the truths of the Holy Scriptures listed above to validate my comments. EVERYTHING we see or touch in this world is spiritual. Everything we say or do is spiritual. Therefore, all things are derived either from the Spirit of God or the spirit of evil, even the very thoughts we receive!

Trying to explain the spiritual world to one unaware of the reality of, or knows not, the Spirit of God, is practically impossible, but I will try. I state this not to imply that I alone know the Spirit of God but rather to assure you of what I do know for certain. It is truly my desire that all of creation could understand God as He really is. When I meet others who know things that I have not yet received, I seek God for added clarity with a desire to know all of Him. Again, I do not question anyone's relationship with God, but I will tell you what I KNOW and have lived since I have personally experienced both sides of the spiritual world. However, I could never have navigated the world of darkness or evil outside the presence of God. Holding my hand so tenderly, I was led daily by the LORD, who continues to provide me with a clear path to a better understanding of His guidance and protectiveness, as expressed in Psalm 23. Here, I am not afraid of the dark, and I know I am surrounded by the light that overpowers the darkness on all sides.

Psalm 23:1-6

[1] The LORD is my shepherd; I shall not want.

² He maketh me to lie down in green pastures: he leadeth me beside the still waters.
³ He restoreth my soul: he leadeth me in the paths of righteousness for his name's sake.
⁴ Yea, though I walk through the valley of the shadow of death, I will fear no evil: for thou art with me; thy rod and thy staff comfort me.
⁵ Thou preparest a table before me in the presence of mine enemies: thou anointest my head with oil; my cup runneth over.
⁶ Surely goodness and mercy shall follow me all the days of my life: and I will dwell in the house of the LORD forever.

Since God dissected my soul, I have been exposed to the spiritual world. From the beginning, Satan has tried to trick me into walking away from "I AM" and following him. I am wise to his many deceptions after being taught personally by Jesus Christ, my Lord. Initially, I recall begging God to take away the teachings and visions of evil that He was introducing me to. Many were simply unbearable! God did not listen to me. He told me that with the work He was calling me to do, I needed to know fully who His enemy is. As I obey Him, His enemy becomes my enemy as well. He said He wanted me to know His enemy as well as I know Him! Soon, it all became commonplace, and fear was removed. This feeling of safety resulted directly from Resting in His Presence!

God gave me great coping resources, including a Spirit of Discernment that allows me to see the enemy with my own eyes, even if he is trying to be invisible. He allows me to detect the presence of evil forces if they are nearby but out of sight, as all evil spirits have a distinct smell. Each smell is unique to the type of spirit involved. The most dangerous spirits are those that have taken possession of a human body!

I realize that some may not believe in the spiritual statements I am presenting. It is OK not to believe. I only ask that you remain open to hearing. God has assured me that if anyone asks Him if my words are valid, He will validate them in such a way that there will be no doubt remaining. So, hear me out, and then go to God in prayer, even if you don't know Him or don't know how to pray, and allow Him to speak the truth to you. You have nothing to lose and everything to gain.

As I began to write this section, "Where do I begin?" I prayed. "LORD God, fill my heart with your Wisdom, as I cannot find words that are adequate to explain the spiritual world. LORD, I don't intend to provide common buzzwords that currently fill thousands of books with everyday, unfounded knowledge of the spiritual world, information based on intellectual beliefs, and a lack of understanding of the scriptures. Help me, Oh God."

It is time for all Believers to rely upon the **wisdom** of the LORD if they believe He truly is God! For too long, the Christian world has developed a God in their minds based on their own understanding. As always, God gave me the best way to explain this powerful area of truth! In obedience, I provide you with various spiritual experiences that I have lived at the will of and in the presence of the LORD. Here, you will understand what it means to operate within the spiritual world as uttered by the Holy Ghost. Be prayerful as you read, and I trust that my LORD will guide your path.

Spiritual Experiences:

Experience #1: He Called Me by Name

The spiritual experience I am recording here occurred while living in Denver, Colorado, and working for a well-known insurance carrier. At the time, I was seriously experiencing medical issues that doctors could not resolve. Excruciating pain in my chest often left me unable to breathe adequately. On that night, I was alone because my husband was out of town for work.

As I prepared to retire for the night, I was very much afraid to go to sleep. I was convinced that if I did so, I would not wake up. I even called a friend and explained what was happening. I asked her to call me early the next day and, if I didn't answer, to come over. My words alarmed her, and she wanted to come over immediately, but I said no. I tried to stay awake as long as I could. I propped the pillows behind me to allow me to sleep without reclining. I was terrified to close my eyes! Suddenly, a bright light appeared in the room.

The brightest light imaginable! It was to my right and rear. It appeared to be a light within a light. From this light, my name was called, "Zelma!" I did not turn to face the light but responded, "Yes, LORD," as I knew this was the voice of God! As His voice spoke, there were rays of light generated that pierced my entire body. Every part of me experienced this indwelling light. The light shone all over the room, and the words spoken were from within this light. My body never turned to face the light or look at it straight on, yet I saw it all. Unexplainable comfort appeared as I was told to lie down and sleep, and that all was well. I again replied, "Yes, LORD." To explain it as "light" is insufficient, but I have no other words.

My life was changed that night. I did not doubt that God was alive and interacting with me! When I awoke, I remembered everything from the night before. It was not a dream or a vision. I had literally heard the voice of God and remembered every detail! I called my sister, living in the area, and excitedly shared with her the experience I had the night before. She was very excited, and we laughed and cried together! She said she, too, believed.

As time passed, I tried to share the experience with everyone I knew, but eventually this stopped. I did not stop learning or believing, but witnessed such hostility and unbelief that I stopped sharing. It was heartbreaking to listen to self-confessing Christians doubt the possibility that God was this real.

Experience #2: A Bomb is About to Go Off

Approximately one year later, an incredible experience occurred in my life. I was learning so much about the LORD, yet there was much still to learn. It was a Sunday morning, and I attended my home church, Union Baptist Church, in Denver, CO. The Pastor was A.L. Bowman. He was a pastor who fought for the civil rights of the people in Denver. To some, his views were very controversial. I was relatively new to the church and did not personally know many of the congregation's members.

This Sunday morning, as the sanctuary started to fill, Pastor Bowman entered the pulpit, accompanied by several police officers who were scattered around the sanctuary. He asked for our attention so he could make an announcement. With a painful look on his face, he informed us there was a bomb threat on the church grounds. He explained that the police officers had searched all buildings and classrooms, and the only possible place left was the sanctuary. Everyone excitedly exhibited alarm as he continued to speak.

Pastor Bowman explained that it could simply be a hoax, or it could be real. He gave us the time that the bomb was supposed to go off. He said that he was not leaving! There were several hundred people in attendance. He explained that he had come to preach and would not leave until he had done so. Many people left immediately. About 30 minutes before the bomb was to explode, he lovingly informed us that each person had to make their own decision and not follow him. I watched as half of the congregation quietly got up and left. Near the 15-minute mark, he again encouraged us to leave if we had any doubts. He began teaching the aspects of personal faith. I remember him saying he would never mention or have hard feelings toward anyone who leaves. Once again, many members left the sanctuary. Within 15 minutes of the anticipated explosion, the entire church was practically empty!

While listening to Pastor Bowman speak, I entered into prayer and found myself in the presence of the LORD. I relived the experience I encountered when He called me by name, as previously explained. Being in the presence of God is not about talking or listening. I can only describe it as "a state of being and knowing." He speaks, but there are no words as we know them, yet words are heard! Being in the presence of God leaves no doubt about what is and what is not.

Instantly, I knew that I was not to leave the church and that it was the perfect will of God for me to remain seated. I did. I heard Pastor Bowman invite everyone to come to the altar for prayer. I obeyed and discovered that only about seven of us were left in the church! As we all knelt at the altar, I noticed that everyone had a visible "halo" around their heads. One of the members later told me that I, too, had a visible halo! We all prayed aloud and remained in prayer for about an hour. After the prayer session, we returned to our seats, and Pastor Bowman began to preach his prepared sermon. Soon, I noticed members who had left earlier started returning to the sanctuary, but many had an apparently broken spirit!

The members who left the church due to the bomb scare had gone across the street to a safe distance to observe what would happen. Once it was determined that the bomb did not explode at the scheduled time, they slowly started to return. Eventually, the sanctuary was filled again, and there was no bomb! At the end of the sermon, another altar call was held. This remaining service was different from any I have ever experienced! Members were seeking the LORD openly and brokenly! During my remaining membership at the church, I never heard Pastor Bowman mention the event. He truly proved to be a man of honor!

Several years later, my family relocated to Illinois. As God was dissecting my soul and appearing to me, He brought all this back to my memory and had me reach out to Pastor Bowman. I called the church, and he answered the phone. I introduced myself, stating that I was one of the members who remained in the church during the bomb scare. He was so glad to hear from me and wanted to know what was happening in my life. I could barely explain, as God was now appearing to me consistently as He was teaching me, as I have described in my testimony. I could only explain that the LORD was in control of my every moment from that day, and he totally understood. My conversation with him was reassuring in so many ways.

Experience #3: Covenants with God Are Sacred

This is another example of the Spiritual Intervention of God in my life. The details of my testimony had already occurred, and I was living to do the will of God as He directed. My husband's mother passed, and we drove from Illinois to Florida for the funeral. My daughter was three years old at the time. On the way there, God entered into a Covenant with me. I did not know much about covenant agreements at the time. Yet, God explained that I would soon need this agreement to be in place for the protection of my family. Not understanding it did not matter as I wanted God to do whatever He chose to in my life.

My husband's family was gathered in the dining room of the family home on the night in question. Suddenly, a loud noise, like a gunshot, exploded within the home. Members fell to the floor while others cried and screamed. The men ran outside to see if the shot had come from outside the home. From my perspective, a great miracle had occurred. A bullet had come through an interior wall inside the house and whisked right by my face and the head of my 3-year-old daughter! Immediately, drywall from the ceiling fell on our heads, and my daughter started to cry. She had just laid her head on my shoulder. Had she not, the bullet would have gone through her head!

We later discovered that one of my brothers-in-law had brought a gun with him. He wrapped it in a blanket and placed it on the top shelf in a bedroom closet. His wife was putting the kids to bed. She grabbed the blanket, and the gun went off, going through the wall into the room where we were all gathered. As the bullet passed my face, I could feel the passing air! Once the men determined what had transpired, everyone was amazed at how the bullet had traveled upwards into the ceiling. When I retired for the evening, with my daughter in my arms, the LORD God appeared. He explained what happened and how it related to the covenant He made with me on the way there.

God explained that Satan had petitioned for me and that He granted his wish! However, He did not allow us to be harmed and told Satan that He had a covenant with me that could not be violated! He explained that Satan was angry because God knew of the covenant before saying yes! I felt so happy, protected, and loved by God.

God further explained that when the bullet approached us, His assigned angel put out His hand, and the bullet bounced off the palm, turned, and went straight up into the ceiling, causing the debris to fall! As amazing as this is to me and witnessed by all the family, when I tried to explain what God said, they failed to believe! This reminds me of the miracles Jesus performed while on earth, which the Israelites witnessed but did not believe. How do I accept the words of such a one who claims to love God and fails to admit what they have personally witnessed?

There are many other examples of the LORD intervening in my life to protect me from harm. Those who believe and know God as God will understand!

Experience #4: Push the Car, Angels

At the beginning of our relationship, Jesus devoted considerable time to ensuring I understood the elements and power of prayer. By so doing, He taught me to love prayer and coming before Him to discuss all things. As my love for worship grew, my love of Jesus Christ also deepened.

One day, while communicating with God, He started to teach me about guardian angels. Once again, He asked if I was using the Guardian Angels assigned to me. What? I pondered! He then explained that angels are assigned to all souls who cry to Him for help. He also said they are not being used by most. I listened intently as He taught me about many of the resources He had assigned to me.

Later that day, while driving my daughter to a Nutcracker rehearsal in downtown Chicago, I noticed that I was almost out of gas. I then turned into a side street I knew had a gas station. Suddenly, I felt the car sputtering as if it was going to stop. I started praying aloud and heard myself repeatedly say, "Push Angels, Push. Push me to the gas station". I even had my young daughter helping me to tell the angels to push. Immediately, a burst of energy hit, and the car sped toward the station! It was propelled to the entrance of the gas station! I was approximately a mile from the entrance when I began to pray. As my car pulled onto the gas station property, it quickly died. Although I was near, I needed to get to the pump, so I went inside the station and asked if they had a gas can I could use. He replied that he had nothing I could put gas in. "Now what?" I thought.

As I spoke with the attendant in the station, I noticed a man shopping inside. He followed me as I walked out of the station towards my car. He asked if I needed help. I explained my problem, and he said he would help. He did not have a gas can, but he told me to get inside the car and put the car in neutral. He then started pushing the car towards a gas pump. He pushed me all the way there! I then got out of the car to thank him and give him a tip. He was nowhere in sight, and the car I saw on the other side of the station was gone. I then asked the station attendant if he had seen which direction the man had gone who was just there. He replied that no one had entered the station except me for over an hour! "No, he was just here and bought items from you when I asked you about the gas can, I exclaimed!" I was totally confused.

When I returned to my car, the LORD began to speak. He told me the man was a guardian angel sent by Him to address my need! He also explained I was not specific in my prayer request, and He gave me what I asked for. He said that because I had only said to push me to the station, that was all I received! I was so humbled and cried profusely. I have since learned to be open and honest with the LORD, telling Him exactly how I feel, even though He already knows my every need. I learned so much from this experience and hold it dearly within my heart.

Experience #5: I Saw Jesus Christ at Wendy's

I know this will sound unreal, but it is one of the clearest things in my mind. While driving to work one day, I stopped at a local Wendy's near me. I didn't understand why, but it was as if I had no control over the decision. When I walked in, I saw a man who appeared to be homeless standing off to the side of the line that had formed. He was very familiar to me, so I walked around him to get a better look at him from the front. He kept turning his body in such a way that I never got a clear look at his face. It appeared he knew my intent and went towards the men's restroom. I got in line to order. I then saw the man at the counter, and he appeared unhappy. As he left the counter, I walked over to him again and asked if I could help in any way. He said no. He explained that He only wanted a large cup of ice. The clerk had given him a medium cup of ice instead. I asked him if I could buy him a large drink, but he declined. The back of His body was so profound and majestic. I knew there was something very special about this man. During this conversation, I kept trying to see his face or look into his eyes! He walked away, leaving me unsuccessful.

When I left the restaurant, he was on the outside talking with another male who also appeared to be trying to address his needs. I walked to my car, feeling very strange inside. Suddenly, I knew the man was Jesus Christ! I was so distraught as I believed I had failed spiritually! I drove around the building, but He was nowhere in sight. I went back inside, but He was not there. As I cried and called out to God to forgive me, He explained that He did not want me to discover who He was at that time. He said that had I been able to look into His eyes, I would have fallen on my knees and acknowledged Him as LORD, and it was not time for this discovery! As the day went on, He assured me I had done well! The key was that I had recognized Him!

I told my Pastor at the time of this encounter, and at first, he appeared to laugh at me, but quickly, his reaction changed to one of pity! He thought I had really lost my mind by saying I saw Jesus Christ at Wendy's. The LORD let me know that he unmercifully mocked me to others as they, too, laughed at me. I was at this church at the will of God and could not leave until the LORD gave me permission to do so. Other members of my family had already found a new church. However, it was after this visit with my Pastor that God allowed me to leave this church. I walked away in so much pain as I had tried desperately to fit in and share the truths the Lord had asked me to share. To this day, I pray fervently for the Ministerial Staff and that Congregation.

Experience #6: Broken Heart Healed by God

God has shown that today's church is trying to play God and

deny His souls the opportunity to personally seek His guidance. If church members fail to follow all the rules set out by the leaders, they are viewed as defiant and insubordinate! The problem arises when such leaders are dictating rules that conflict with the instructions of God.

Completely understanding my commandments from God made it difficult for me to conform to any congregation. Yet, I longed to be a part of a loving fellowship willing to obey the LORD. God knew this desire of my heart while knowing it would never work!

He took me to a church that was seeking a new Pastor. The congregation chose a young pastor that was not the choice of the departing founding Pastor. There was great turmoil between the two. The LORD showed me the problems that existed within the church that provided spiritual conflict to the detriment of them both.

The LORD gave me a message for them both to give me spiritual standing with these men. I was new at the church, and neither knew me nor had any reason to listen to me. As I approached each Pastor, I was not turned away. I met with them twice individually and once as a group. After this meeting, as I presented God's warnings, there was a reconciliation among the group. Subsequently, God revealed that there was still a problem within the hearts.

Believing this could be the perfect church home for me and my family, we united with this congregation. The harmony and peace were soon shattered as I began to speak the truths required by the LORD. The more I tried not to say, the more the warnings came forth! Finally, I was soon an outcast among the 24+ Ministerial Staff. The Pastor took away all speaking opportunities, and the entire congregation knew of this decision. It was so humiliating!

One night, as I sat in a Revival that was beginning that night, I experienced "heartbreak" that led to death! The Pastor had done something that hurt me so badly that my heart literally broke. I gave up and asked God to bring me home. Everything within me changed. I knew that I no longer existed. I don't know how to explain this pain, but it was real. Then I felt the touch of the LORD, and I was alive again. He told me that it was not time for me to depart as much work was needed. He informed me Satan was in the building and true worshippers and prayers were needed. I can never casually speak of a broken heart after this incident. The LORD let me know that my heart had truly broken, and His love restored it.

Experience #7: Worldly Strong Men

Several years ago, I had a dream that troubled me greatly. I saw many men and women gathered at a Great Table. They were very familiar with each other. They represented different countries. These men controlled all the wealth, crime, and evil in the world. They had been meeting for decades. They had developed a plan to implement their final strategy for reorganizing the world as a whole. I listened to their conversation in shock. When the dream ended, I went to God in prayer, seeking an explanation of what I saw and heard. God did not explain and told me to wait. During the writing of this book, the LORD focused my attention again on this dream and asked if I now understood. As I reflect on the day's events, everything becomes spiritually clear! I pray that you have ears to hear "What Thus Saith the Lord God," Amen.

~ 22 ~

Prayer Is the Answer

> *¹⁰ I was in the Spirit on the Lord's day, and heard behind me a great voice, as of a trumpet,*
> *¹¹ Saying, I am Alpha and Omega, the first and the last: and, What thou seest, write in a book, and send it unto the seven churches which are in Asia; unto Ephesus, and unto Smyrna, and unto Pergamos, and unto Thyatira, and unto Sardis, and unto Philadelphia, and unto Laodicea. ~ Revelation 1:10-11*

No man can know God without communicating with Him. Prayer is simply talking to God. It doesn't have to be vocal; it's often more genuine when expressed from the heart. Since God is a Spirit, we MUST worship Him with our spirit and be truthful! There is no alternate way of loving and worshiping Him.

> *But the hour cometh, and now is, when the true worshippers shall worship the Father in spirit and in truth: for the Father seeketh such to worship him. ~ John 4:23*

God is a Spirit: and they that worship him must worship him in spirit and in truth. ~ *John 4:24*

Even Apostle John received the mystery of the sea through revelatory prayer. Please remember that Satan cannot read your mind! He can only put thoughts within your mind, hoping you will listen and follow him rather than God. God alone knows our inner thoughts and beliefs until we voice them aloud. This creates a path for us to talk to the LORD truthfully in privacy. It was through this avenue that Apostle John received the revelations from God and knew how to move forward.

People often say that prayer changes things, and this is true. However, we must admit that God hears and responds to the prayers of the righteous in the heart. A most famous scripture that many so- called Christians recite is 2 Chronicles 7:14. There is more to the scripture that must be understood. First, know that God was responding to the prayer presented by King Solomon after he had completed the New Temple built for the LORD God. Solomon petitioned the LORD to not forget the repentant prayers of the people. Please read 2 Chronicles 6: 14-42 to understand all the details of Solomon's request to the LORD. After reading his prayer, you will better understand the response from the LORD, as stated below. Know that God provided a blessing if they truly repented and a cursing if He was forsaken:

2 Chronicles 7:11-22

[11] Thus Solomon finished the house of the LORD, and the king's house: and all that came into Solomon's heart to make in the house of the LORD, and in his own house, he prosperously effected.
[12] And the LORD appeared to Solomon by night, and said unto him, I have heard thy prayer, and have chosen this place to myself for an house of sacrifice.
[13] If I shut up heaven that there be no rain, or if I command the locusts to devour the land, or if I send pestilence among my people;
[14] If my people, which are called by my name, shall humble themselves, and pray, and seek my face, and turn from their wicked ways; then will I hear from heaven, and will forgive their sin, and will heal their land.
[15] Now mine eyes shall be open, and mine ears attent unto the prayer that is made in this place.
[16] For now have I chosen and sanctified this house, that my name may be there for ever: and mine eyes and mine heart shall be there perpetually.
[17] And as for thee, if thou wilt walk before me, as David thy father walked, and do according

to all that I have commanded thee, and shalt observe my statutes and my judgments;
¹⁸ Then will I stablish the throne of thy kingdom, according as I have covenanted with David thy father, saying, There shall not fail thee a man to be ruler in Israel.
¹⁹ But if ye turn away, and forsake my statutes and my commandments, which I have set before you, and shall go and serve other gods, and worship them;
²⁰ Then will I pluck them up by the roots out of my land which I have given them; and this house, which I have sanctified for my name, will I cast out of my sight, and will make it to be a proverb and a byword among all nations.
²¹ And this house, which is high, shall be an astonishment to every one that passeth by it; so that he shall say, Why hath the LORD done thus unto this land, and unto this house?
²² And it shall be answered, Because they forsook the LORD God of their fathers, which brought them forth out of the land of Egypt, and laid hold on other gods, and worshipped them, and served them: therefore hath he brought all this evil upon them.

Although God provides a HUGE promise in the preceding scriptures, it is for those who love and follow His commands. The promise I am speaking of results from the mighty prayer offered by Solomon after completing the construction of the temple dedicated to the LORD that his father David had commissioned.

Solomon knew the sinfulness of the hearts of Judah and Israel, so he asked God to forgive the people for an assortment of sins if, afterwards, they repented and changed their ways. The Lord God listened carefully and promised Solomon that if the people would humble themselves before Him in prayer and stop sinning, He would forgive them! This also makes it clear that those not abiding by the LORD have no guarantee that their prayers will be heard! It also means that the LORD is anticipating a change of heart and obedience from us all to His current charge regarding our sinfulness.

Prayer is the absolute answer to all wrongs in the world. We can never find peace and understanding without praying to the only Living God Almighty. The Holy Scriptures are filled with prayers of many types, such as Thanksgiving, Praise, Repentance, Worship, Victory, and Blessings, to name a few. I believe the Book of Psalms contains more prayers than any other book, although I have not verified this claim. However, the most impactful prayer upon my heart was when Jesus prayed to the Father in the Garden of Gethsemane.

Mark 14:32-42

³² And they came to a place which was named Gethsemane: and he saith to his disciples, Sit ye here, while I shall pray.
³³ And he taketh with him Peter and James and John, and began to be sore amazed, and to be very heavy;
³⁴ And saith unto them, My soul is exceeding sorrowful unto death: tarry ye here, and watch.
³⁵ And he went forward a little, and fell on the ground, and prayed that, if it were possible, the hour might pass from him.
³⁶ And he said, Abba, Father, all things are possible unto thee; take away this cup from me: nevertheless not what I will, but what thou wilt. ³⁷ And he cometh, and findeth them sleeping, and saith unto Peter, Simon, sleepest thou? couldest not thou watch one hour?
³⁸ Watch ye and pray, lest ye enter into temptation. The spirit truly is ready, but the flesh is weak.
³⁹ And again he went away, and prayed, and spake the same words.
⁴⁰ And when he returned, he found them asleep again, (for their eyes were heavy,) neither wist they what to answer him.
⁴¹ And he cometh the third time, and saith unto them, Sleep on now, and take your rest: it is enough, the hour is come; behold, the Son of man is betrayed into the hands of sinners.
⁴² Rise up, let us go; lo, he that betrayeth me is at hand.

I have heard many discussions of Mark 14:32-42 but never have I heard what I see and understand about this scripture as I rest in the presence of the LORD. Allow me to show you what I see and hear.

Jesus was constantly teaching his disciples how to live according to the true beliefs of the LORD, which always included prayer. Now, if you believe that God is truly God, as I do, have you ever considered the actual words and actions Jesus took as He prayed in Mark 14? Verse 33 says when He selected Peter, James, and John to go pray with Him, He began to be sore, amazed, and very heavy. Although the words "sore, amazed, and heavy" are ordinary, the LORD did not accept my original understanding of them. As I studied further, I discovered meanings like terrified, disgusted, horrified, and distressed of mind that offered insight into what He was feeling!

1. He became internally distraught and said to them, "My soul is exceeding sorrowful unto death."

2. Tarry ye here, and watch.

Can you imagine Our Lord being distressed, or terrified, and "sorrowful unto death"? He asked them to Tarry and Watch. They did neither! As He prayed to the Father, He asked if the cup could be removed from Him if possible. Jesus was sent to earth to shed His blood on the cross, enabling mankind to live and prevail over evil through repentance and prayer. The Lord knew what was at stake. Are we to believe He was willing to alter the Master Plan of God for His own sake? It does not matter that He wanted this alteration only if it was the will of God! My spirit tells me that this was not about Jesus Himself but was all about the Disciples. His prayer was for the disciples and not Himself! This explains why they were told to "tarry, watch, and pray." Three times, He checked on them, and each time, they had fallen asleep! He even warned them that they would succumb to temptation unless they stayed awake to pray! After the third time, He just said, "Sleep on now and take your rest." He knew that their flesh alone was too weak to fight the attacks of Satan.

What was really happening? Jesus knew that Satan would attack His disciples during and after His crucifixion. He knew Peter, James, and John were the leaders, and the other disciples would follow whatever they did. He even warned Peter of his upcoming attack. Jesus Christ, the Lord, prayed so intently and fervently for His Disciples that the scriptures state that His sweat was as blood!

Luke 22:39-46

[39] And he came out, and went, as he was wont, to the mount of Olives; and his disciples also followed him.
[40] And when he was at the place, he said unto them, Pray that ye enter not into temptation.
[41] And he was withdrawn from them about a stone's cast, and kneeled down, and prayed,
[42] Saying, Father, if thou be willing, remove this cup from me: nevertheless not my will, but thine, be done.
[43] And there appeared an angel unto him from heaven, strengthening him.
[44] And being in an agony he prayed more earnestly: and his sweat was as it were great drops of blood falling down to the ground.
[45] And when he rose up from prayer, and was come to his disciples, he found them sleeping for sorrow,
[46] And said unto them, Why sleep ye? rise and pray, lest ye enter into temptation.

WHAT A PRAYER! Jesus prays no less today for us all and continues to push us toward understanding that His Love for us is never-ending. Sometimes, the Father allows us to endure what appear to be terrible circumstances so we can gain the truth about prayer and repentance.

~ 23 ~

Stir Up the Spirit of God

> *²⁹ And Jesus answered him, The first of all the commandments is, Hear, O Israel; The Lord our God is one Lord:*
> *³⁰ And thou shalt love the Lord thy God with all thy heart, and with all thy soul, and with all thy mind, and with all thy strength: this is the first commandment.*
> *³¹ And the second is like, namely this, Thou shalt love thy neighbour as thyself. There is none other commandment greater than these. ~ Mark 12:29-31*

The soul of all mankind is created always to be "stirred up" by the Holy Ghost and in love with Jesus Christ and the LORD God Almighty! Until this "stirring" takes place within the human spirit of mankind, there can be no true love for God generated from the soul of man. When the Holy Ghost stirs the spirit of man, there develops a spiritual connection with the Spirit of God. Without this spiritual connection, humankind cannot create an intimate relationship with the LORD God Almighty.

With the stirring of the spirit of man, and the subsequent union with the Spirit of God, Spirit-to-spirit Connection, the soul falls into submission to the human spirit of man, which has been connected to the very Spirit of God Almighty. NOW WE HAVE UNION WITH GOD... and the means to crucify the flesh! The commandment of our Lord and Savior is clear as expressed in the scriptures below:

Romans 8:8-17

[8] So then they that are in the flesh cannot please God.
[9] But ye are not in the flesh, but in the Spirit, if so be that the Spirit of God dwell in you. Now if any man have not the Spirit of Christ, he is none of his.
[10] And if Christ be in you, the body is dead because of sin; but the Spirit is life because of righteousness.
[11] But if the Spirit of him that raised up Jesus from the dead dwell in you, he that raised up Christ from the dead shall also quicken your mortal bodies by his Spirit that dwelleth in you. [12] Therefore, brethren, we are debtors, not to the flesh, to live after the flesh.
[13] For if ye live after the flesh, ye shall die: but if ye through the Spirit do mortify the deeds of the body, ye shall live.

¹⁴ For as many as are led by the Spirit of God, they are the sons of God.

¹⁵ For ye have not received the spirit of bondage again to fear; but ye have received the Spirit of adoption, whereby we cry, Abba, Father.
¹⁶ The Spirit itself beareth witness with our spirit, that we are the children of God:
¹⁷ And if children, then heirs; heirs of God, and joint-heirs with Christ; if so be that we suffer with him, that we may be also glorified together.

¹⁶ This I say then, Walk in the Spirit, and ye shall not fulfil the lust of the flesh. ¹⁷ For the flesh lusteth against the Spirit, and the Spirit against the flesh: and these are contrary the one to the other: so that ye cannot do the things that ye would. ~ Galatians 5:16-17

²⁴ And they that are Christ's have crucified the flesh with the affections and lusts. ~ Galatians 5:24

² That he no longer should live the rest of his time in the flesh to the lusts of men, but to the will of God. ~ 1 Peter 4:2

Spiritual Challenge: Get to KNOW "I AM"

As evidenced by the referenced scriptures above, there MUST be a connection between the human spirit of man and the Spirit of God. When this spiritual connection occurs, the flesh of the body dies and succumbs to the power and Spirit of the LORD. I have included multiple scriptures for review and could have added others. My goal is to show that this is not an optional choice but a spiritual battle for the soul of man that can only be overcome by the spiritual power of the LORD. God protects us from His enemy because He loves us. He desires that we return His love. There is no explanation for the incredible love God extends to His followers.

Our entire perspective of the world changes when we understand that God is Love and Satan is evil. There is no question as to His love for all souls created. The real question is...Do WE love Him? My response is Yes. If your answer is Yes, does He know it? Can the people around you see your love for God clearly in the life you live? Have YOU allowed the Holy Ghost to **"stir up"** the Love of God in your heart for all to see? Have you EVER met **I AM** as the only Almighty God? Are you able to access the Throne of God? Are you willing to fall madly **and radically in**

love with Jesus Christ? Do you want to build a stronger relationship with the Lord Jesus? If your answer is yes to any of these questions, and you truly want more, no one can stand in your way!

There is so much more to knowing, understanding, trusting, and obeying the LORD God Almighty (**I AM**). There is so much more to understanding the true, pure, holy nature of **I AM**. Through the Wisdom of the Holy Ghost, we gain the correct understanding of who **I AM** is. This Wisdom elucidates that there is MORE! Biblical scriptures document that Adam and Eve became the first trusted vessels of "More." Noah discovered "More." Moses was taught that there was "More." Abraham found "More." Ezekiel was shown "More." King Solomon was entrusted with understanding the concept of "More." Daniel became aware of "More." In his zealousness for righteousness, Paul discovered there was "More." And John, on the Island of Patmos, came face to face with "More."

Throughout the scriptures, both Old and New Testaments, God has consistently pleaded to mankind to get to know all of Him. He wants us to love Him above all else. See the scriptures below and see what God is saying.

And thou shalt love the Lord thy God with all thine heart, and with all thy soul, and with all thy might. ~ *Deuteronomy 6:5*

And now, Israel, what doth the Lord thy God require of thee, but to fear the Lord thy God, to walk in all his ways, and to love him, and to serve the Lord thy God with all thy heart and with all thy soul, ~ *Deuteronomy 10:12*

And it shall come to pass, if ye shall hearken diligently unto my commandments which I command you this day, to love the Lord your God, and to serve him with all your heart and with all your soul, ~ *Deuteronomy 11:13*

Thou shalt not hearken unto the words of that prophet, or that dreamer of dreams: for the Lord your God proveth you, to know whether ye love the Lord your God with all your heart and with all your soul. ~ *Deuteronomy 13:3*

And the Lord thy God will circumcise thine heart, and the heart of thy seed, to love the Lord thy God with all thine heart, and with all thy soul, that thou mayest live. ~ *Deuteronomy 30:6*

But take diligent heed to do the commandment and the law, which Moses the servant of the

Lord charged you, to love the Lord your God, and to walk in all his ways, and to keep his commandments, and to cleave unto him, and to serve him with all your heart and with all your soul. ~ Joshua 22:5

And Samuel spake unto all the house of Israel, saying, If ye do return unto the Lord with all your hearts, then put away the strange gods and Ashtaroth from among you, and prepare your hearts unto the Lord, and serve him only: and he will deliver you out of the hand of the Philistines.
~ 1 Samuel 7:3

And Samuel said unto the people, Fear not: ye have done all this wickedness: yet turn not aside from following the Lord, but serve the Lord with all your heart; ~ 1 Samuel 12:20

Only fear the Lord, and serve him in truth with all your heart: for consider how great things he hath done for you. ~ 1 Samuel 12:24

I will praise thee, O Lord, with my whole heart; I will shew forth all thy marvellous works.
~ Psalm 9:1

Praise ye the Lord. I will praise the Lord with my whole heart, in the assembly of the upright, and in the congregation. ~ Psalm 111:1

Blessed are they that keep his testimonies, and that seek him with the whole heart. ~ Psalm 119:2

With my whole heart have I sought thee: O let me not wander from thy commandments. ~ Psalm 119:10

Give me understanding, and I shall keep thy law; yea, I shall observe it with my whole heart. ~ Psalm 119:34

I intreated thy favour with my whole heart: be merciful unto me according to thy word. ~ Psalm 119:58

The proud have forged a lie against me: but I will keep thy precepts with my whole heart. ~ Psalm 119:69

I cried with my whole heart; hear me, O Lord: I will keep thy statutes. ~ Psalm 119:145

I will praise thee with my whole heart: before the gods will I sing praise unto thee. ~ Psalm 138:1

And yet for all this her treacherous sister Judah hath not turned unto me with her whole heart, but feignedly, saith the Lord. ~ Jeremiah 3:10

And I will give them an heart to know me, that I am the Lord: and they shall be my people, and I will be their God: for they shall return unto me with their whole heart. ~ Jeremiah 24:7

And ye shall seek me, and find me, when ye shall search for me with all your heart. ~ Jeremiah 29:13

Therefore also now, saith the Lord, turn ye even to me with all your heart, and with fasting, and with weeping, and with mourning: ~ Joel 2:12

Jesus said unto him, Thou shalt love the Lord thy God with all thy heart, and with all thy soul, and with all thy mind. ~ Matthew 22:37

And thou shalt love the Lord thy God with all thy heart, and with all thy soul, and with all thy mind, and with all thy strength: this is the first commandment. ~ Mark 12:30

And he answering said, Thou shalt love the Lord thy God with all thy heart, and with all thy soul, and with all thy strength, and with all thy mind; and thy neighbour as thyself. ~ Luke 10:27

As another reference and reminder of the desired submission to the LORD, consider the scripture below:

I am crucified with Christ: nevertheless I live; yet not I, but Christ liveth in me: and the life which I now live in the flesh I live by the faith of the Son of God, who loved me, and gave himself for me. ~ Galatians 2:20

I encourage you to discover the true, everlasting power and love of Jesus. I intend to move forward fervently to engage the whole world with God's message. I know that His message of love applies to all, including me. My goal is to unite true believers worldwide, bringing them together from the North, the South, the East, and the West. Will you help me shift the conversation from constantly acknowledging the evil spreading throughout the universe to "Resting in the presence of the LORD?" This is my goal. This is my charge from God Almighty. Amen.

~ 24 ~

Evil Has No Face

> *The fear of the LORD is to hate evil: pride, and arrogancy, and the evil way, and the froward mouth, do I hate. ~ Proverbs 8:13*
>
> *Beloved, follow not that which is evil, but that which is good. He that doeth good is of God: but he that doeth evil hath not seen God. ~ 3 John 1:11*

No man can naturally discern evil without spiritual discernment received directly from the LORD. Yet again, Satan has redefined the meaning of spiritual discernment. This alteration by evil forces was presented to mankind to give the impression that even false believers have spiritual discernment! True spiritual discernment sees the invisible, unknown things, as well as those visible to the natural eye. It is not a hunch or a feeling. This gift is granted only at the will of the Lord. One of the benefits of resting in the Presence of the Lord is to know deceitfulness when it appears. Evil also recognizes righteousness when it is present.

Due to the impact of evil upon humankind, it is almost impossible to determine which spirit is before you. As God has said, goodness is not enough. Many good men have missed the mark as they deceive the world about the condition of their hearts, which is the only thing that matters. A good man can be persuaded to abandon or not accept the ways of the LORD. However, a soul resting in the presence of the Lord goes to God for direction to avoid being deceived. Therefore, be aware of who is leading you. Don't trust anyone except the LORD. He will never deceive you or allow you to be deceived without His knowledge! He will always be with you wherever you go.

There are so many events within the Holy Scriptures that will provide understanding and discernment of the spiritual nature of darkness within the Sea if you search with an open mind to know the truth. Look at the Red Sea that stood before the Israelites as they escaped the bondage of Egypt at the will of God while guided by Moses. The people panicked as Pharaoh and his army approached from the rear, and the Sea before them cut off all escape routes from the impending threat. Moses helplessly prayed and sought God for help! Imagine the uncertainty in the heart of Moses as he was being told to raise the Rod God had given him and then walk straight through the waters of the Sea! Yet Moses obeyed this command in faith and trusting that God was in control. Suddenly, everyone could see the water rising high in the air, creating a dry path to cross to the other side.

Pharaoh and his men witnessed this act and, in response, followed the people of God into the waters of the sea! Immediately, the waters receded and covered all men and horses other than Moses and the Israelites! Moses was shown again the greatness of God's powers through prayer. With your new understanding that the Sea is evil, hopefully, you can see that Satan had to obey Moses as he followed the righteousness and power of God. Every book in the Bible references the Sea and its evil nature.

While you consider the evilness of the sea, which man plays with and cherishes every day, do not forget that the Earth, too, is evil! By earth, I mean the dry land upon which we walk, build, and play! The deep waters that God called Seas and the Dry Land that He called Earth were originally the same! He commanded the Sea to stay in its lane, and He placed mankind on dry land or the Earth. Satan can only be granted the privilege of leaving his designated home of evil if he finds a body to occupy where the soul has not surrendered to the LORD! This is how he and his demons are capturing the hearts and minds of mankind. When hurricanes come upon the earth, much evil is let loose, and many are possessed by these evil forces that are looking for bodies in which they can live "OUT OF THE SEA." Anyone who has ears to hear and understand what I mean, please listen to me!

One more thing about the Sea and the Earth. The Crude oil that we drill from beneath the Earth and Sea is the actual bloodline of evil that God confined to the Sea in the Book of Genesis! The world believes that riches and gain are received by those who have the most oil! Wherever there is oil…there are substantial evil spirits and domination of the soul of man. The same evil applies to underground minerals that are being taken from beneath the earth. Due to the ignorance of the world, we now develop and establish our economies based on the amount of crude oil. It provides heat for our homes and other resources that we now deem as necessities. Man prides himself on his great inventions of the world, but God is not impressed. Let's view what God has to say about these resources that we believe are so great:

Thou answeredst them, O LORD our God: thou wast a God that forgavest them, though thou tookest vengeance of their inventions. ~ Psalms 99:8

Thus they provoked him to anger with their inventions: and the plague brake in upon them. ~ Psalms 106:29

Thus were they defiled with their own works, and went a whoring with their own inventions. ~ Psalms 106:39

I wisdom dwell with prudence, and find out knowledge of witty inventions. ~ Proverbs 8:12

Lo, this only have I found, that God hath made man upright; but they have sought out many inventions. ~ Ecclesiastes 7:29

When you consider the scriptures above, it is clear that the LORD is not impressed with our inventions on earth, as He knows that we are clueless to the many truths that are plainly before us. Study the Book of Ecclesiastes for an in-depth understanding of how dreadful the Sea and Earth are! When

Solomon was faced with the knowledge as I have presented in this writing, he cried out to God and exclaimed, "What's the point as everything I do is in vain. It's ALL vanity of vanities." *(Paraphrased)*

Never doubt the love and protection of the LORD! He will always be there to protect all souls, but there is special protection for those who love Him in return. Listen, therefore, to the **"change"** that the Lord is asking of us. Allow Him to draw you closer to His bosom until you can say:

"I found Him whom my soul loves."
Song of Solomon 3:40

~ 25 ~

Modern-Day Pharisees

> *For I say unto you, That except your righteousness shall exceed the righteousness of the scribes and Pharisees, ye shall in no case enter into the kingdom of heaven. ~ Matthew 5:20*
>
> *Woe unto you, scribes and Pharisees, hypocrites! for ye compass sea and land to make one proselyte, and when he is made, ye make him twofold more the child of hell than yourselves. ~ Matthew 23:15*

Our LORD says His heart is broken over the actions and teachings of the Christian World, but this pain goes much deeper when He considers the abominable actions of today's church leaders. "They have no shame when corrupting the house of God. They fear no one with the lies they teach and believe that they themselves are in total control. They set themselves on high and live lavish lives at the expense of the church body while the poor among them is daily hurting and crying for help," Thus saith the Lord God. "How long will they treat me like an idol god, Saith the LORD? Do they have no shame? Do they think they are invisible to my eyes that see all things and ears that hear all things? Time is running out, and I will not wait much longer," Saith the Lord.

Most bible students know how disgusting the Pharisees and Sadducees were to Jesus Christ. He often referred to them as hypocrites! This means they were teaching or demanding things of others that they themselves were guilty of. I ask that such leaders seek clarification from God to determine if He is speaking of you. Do not assume that all is well with you and the Lord! I know you recall the message Prophet Nathan delivered to King David after he sinned against God, reminding the people that God's eyes could see every action and thought. He paid greatly for this deception against the LORD.

2 Samuel 12: 8-14:

⁸ And I gave thee thy master's house, and thy master's wives into thy bosom, and gave thee the house of Israel and of Judah; and if that had been too little, I would moreover have given unto thee such and such things.

> *⁹ Wherefore hast thou despised the commandment of the LORD, to do evil in his sight? thou hast killed Uriah the Hittite with the sword, and hast taken his wife to be thy wife, and hast slain him with the sword of the children of Ammon.*
> *¹⁰ Now therefore the sword shall never depart from thine house; because thou hast despised me, and hast taken the wife of Uriah the Hittite to be thy wife.*
> *¹¹ Thus saith the LORD, Behold, I will raise up evil against thee out of thine own house, and I will take thy wives before thine eyes, and give them unto thy neighbour, and he shall lie with thy wives in the sight of this sun.*
> *¹² For thou didst it secretly: but I will do this thing before all Israel, and before the sun.*
> *¹³ And David said unto Nathan, I have sinned against the LORD. And Nathan said unto David, The LORD also hath put away thy sin; thou shalt not die.*
> *¹⁴ Howbeit, because by this deed thou hast given great occasion to the enemies of the LORD to blaspheme, the child also that is born unto thee shall surely die.*

Are you willing to continue to rebel against Almighty God? Repent as David did and save your soul. According to the Lord, leaders today are involved in secret sexual activities and many other abominable acts that raise a great stench to the Throne of

God! Amen.

It is a great honor for those called by God to teach and present the Gospel of the Lord to the world! However, it is abominable to teach falsely and cause harm to the people of God! The LORD says He is not going to wait much longer! I am not sure what this means, but He made a similar statement when addressing the people in Noah's day.

<u>Genesis 6:5-7</u>

⁵ And GOD saw that the wickedness of man was great in the earth, and that every imagination of the thoughts of his heart was only evil continually.
⁶ And it repented the LORD that he had made man on the earth, and it grieved him at his heart. ⁷ And the LORD said, I will destroy man whom I have created from the face of the earth; both man, and beast, and the creeping thing, and the fowls of the air; for it repenteth me that I have made them.

~ 26 ~

"There Is More to This Thing Called Love" Thus Saith the LORD God Almighty

> *Dear LORD, my God, the great "I AM That I AM," I honor you today as my Savior and my forever Friend. You are my All and All. You are the best friend I ever had! I love you with my whole heart, my mind, my soul, my might, and all my strength! Help me Father to endure to the end! Thanks for teaching me to Love you as I do yet while knowing there is so much more to learn. Amen.*

True Love is everlasting. It never fades away or makes excuses for any possible mistakes that occur. It does not hold us in bondage to each other and never abuses us. It never lies to us. True love watches over us and is always prepared to personally suffer pain and loss so that we might survive or succeed at all costs. All people need true love! However, we must first be willing to practice and give true love!

I found true Love when I met Jesus Christ! No one has ever pierced my heart as Jesus has, breathed so sweetly upon my face, or spoken so firmly yet so tenderly with unspeakable love. The more they (Father, Son, and Holy Ghost) expressed their love for me through their actions and guidance, the more I loved them. They made me feel safe and confident in every situation I faced. Shortly after discovering this magnificent love, I found myself saying that no one loves them as much as I do! I purposed in my heart that all of me had to belong to God. To this day, even in my teaching, I declare that no one loves the LORD as much as I do! I am not ashamed to profess my love. I recall a relative asking me why there was a competition. I never considered it a competition, so I responded that my statements were about me and my personal relationship with My LORD. Everyone can love as much or even more than I do! It is an individual decision.

I'm still declaring my love this way and praying that I always will. As the years passed, our love increased, and God validated the love I was expressing. Subsequently, He began to teach me more about love and declared, *"There is more to this thing called Love."* I did not understand and sought answers to what was meant by this statement. When I did not get an answer right away, I continued to pray and search the Scriptures. There is a difference between finding one or two scripture references that support one's view on a particular matter and finding multiple references that are undeniably clear regarding the expectations of Father God Almighty. The Holy Scriptures clarify that God expects us to return Their[8] love.

> *And shewing mercy unto thousands of them that love me, and keep my commandments.*
> *~ Exodus 20:6*

> *And shewing mercy unto thousands of them that love me and keep my commandments.*
> *~ Deuteronomy 5:10*

> **I love them that love me; and those that seek me early shall find me. ~ Proverbs 8:17**
> *(Emphasis added)*

> *That I may cause those that love me to inherit substance; and I will fill their treasures.*
> *~ Proverbs 8:21*

> *He hath shewed thee, O man, what is good; and what doth the LORD require of thee, but to do*

---

[8] 'Their' (here I am referring to Father God, Jesus Christ, and the Holy Ghost)

justly, and to love mercy, and to walk humbly with thy God? ~ Micah 6:8

Jesus said unto them, If God were your Father, ye would love me: for I proceeded forth and came from God; neither came I of myself, but he sent me. ~ John 8:42

If ye love me, keep my commandments. ~ John 14:15

Jesus answered and said unto him, If a man love me, he will keep my words: and my Father will love him, and we will come unto him, and make our abode with him. ~ John 14:23

Proverbs 8:17 even states that God loves those who love Him! It is now time for all souls who claim to love the LORD to seek Him with all their hearts! Don't leave anything to chance. We have nothing to lose by pressing harder to love the Lord with our whole hearts. I will continue to use all my strength to pursue every ounce of His love forever and always! "Please help me to love you more and more, dear LORD, is my prayer." Amen.

Ultimately, the LORD began to show me what He meant by saying, "There is more to this thing called love." I will only state some of these lessons here. It also becomes an individualized learning experience. But I do pray that you will ask for understanding in your life and walk with Him.

Jesus Christ continuously tells us to love each other and help those in need. This is specifically stated in scripture.9 To perfect my love for others, I was thrown into the fire to measure my love for others that I was expressing with my mouth. God taught me how to adequately respond to the needs of the homeless or those in domestic danger, even if it meant bringing them into my home to survive.

Over a six-month period, my family provided shelter in my home and financial assistance to at least six adults! There was no choice and no pain, as God specifically told me what to do and how to do it. Several of them were obviously demon-possessed, and others were being clearly manipulated to perform actions on behalf of evil. To this day, one of those souls still resides in my home with us. She had been diagnosed with Schizophrenia and Bipolar Depression disorders and came to our home directly from a

---

[9] Proverbs 19:17 CEB states that "Those who are gracious to the poor lend to the LORD, and the LORD will fully repay them"

mental institution. She also suffered from drug and alcohol abuse. Life each day was unpredictable, at best. The LORD, in His Wisdom, did not allow me to go anywhere without her. She joined me at my church services and social events. Even out-of-town business trips were included. I also accompanied her on all her doctor visits. This created a bond that, over time, became very strong. Yet, I often felt trapped, thinking there would never be any relief, all while knowing this was God's perfect plan!

About two years into providing a home for this soul, God clarified it was now time for me to love her. I thought I was already expressing love! I was making a huge sacrifice for her. God kept telling me I needed to love her! As I surrendered my heart to love her truly and completely, I noticed significant changes in her personality. Day by day, I watched the LORD transform her spirit. My granddaughter, who was two years old, would not go near her. Little by little, the demonic activity ceased to be obvious! Then, one day, she seemed free of all demonic influences. The LORD helped me to understand that "Love" had set her free! He explained that evil cannot love on any level and will immediately flee in the presence of true love. This, however, only results after true submission to the Lord.

Submit yourselves therefore to God. Resist the devil, and he will flee from you. ~ James 4:7

Humble yourselves in the sight of the Lord, and he shall lift you up. ~ James 4:10

Do you get this? Demons cannot remain within the body of anyone in the presence of LOVE! The only genuine exorcism of evil spirits is Love! During the aftermath of this spiritual change, I poured the truths of God into her spirit daily. Although she periodically struggles, she has greatly advanced as a student. Yet, I am very cautious as I know that unless she continues to be one with Christ, those evil spirits can return. Without knowing that we were seeking the face and guidance of the LORD, her doctors declared her healed from all mental illness and took her off all medications! Have you ever heard of those with Bipolar Depression NOT being required to take medication to live normally? Loving God is the answer to all worldly and spiritual problems. Amen.

There is no way to read what is written while seeking the truth from God and ignoring the fact that God wants our hearts completely. He goes further by declaring that "the whole heart" must be given and surrendered in true love.

But if from thence thou shalt seek the LORD thy God, thou shalt find him, if thou seek him with all thy heart and with all thy soul. ~ Deuteronomy 4:29

And now, Israel, what doth the LORD thy God require of thee, but to fear the LORD thy God, to walk in all his ways, and to love him, and to serve the LORD thy God with all thy heart and with all thy soul, ~ Deuteronomy 10:12

Jesus said unto him, Thou shalt love the Lord thy God with all thy heart, and with all thy soul, and with all thy mind. ~ Matthew 22:37

And thou shalt love the Lord thy God with all thy heart, and with all thy soul, and with all thy mind, and with all thy strength: this is the first commandment. ~ Mark 12:30

From the beginning of time, the LORD has sought the hearts of mankind, so yes, I purposed to go further than anyone I knew or had heard of. These scriptures strengthened me to press hard to surrender my whole heart to my Lord and my God! My goal was and continues to be resting in His presence always, while maintaining a Radical love relationship! Please read the scriptures listed above to see how God has always asked us to love Him and obey his commands.

Section IV

Minister McKinney's Take on it All

~ 27 ~

What Does It All Mean?

> ³ *Jesus answered and said unto him, Verily, verily, I say unto thee, Except a man be born again, he cannot see the kingdom of God.*
> ⁴ *Nicodemus saith unto him, How can a man be born when he is old? can he enter the second time into his mother's womb, and be born?*
> ⁵ *Jesus answered, Verily, verily, I say unto thee, Except a man be born of water and of the Spirit, he cannot enter into the kingdom of God. ~ John 3:3-5*

Time is running out to accept God's love and obey His commands. As I read the biblical scriptures, I am always amazed at the degree of rejection of God's teachings that were presented to Israel. How could they not see what was clearly before them? Now, I get it. The same situations are happening today, and the world is again not listening or willing to obey the LORD.

A war is going on. The worldly spirits of evil are fighting against the spiritual forces of God! Everyone wants to be right in their opinion without seeking the Wisdom of God. People are fighting over abortions and reproductive health care, gay and lesbian issues, voting rights, political violence, democracy, autocracy, and racial issues, just to name a few. I don't see God in any of the arguments I hear, and I feel so very sad for our world. This emotion is present, especially for those of us who claim to be Christians! We are warned in scripture to try the spirit by the SPIRIT of God. We know that Satan is a liar and the father of lies, as shown in John 8: 42-47 below:

John **8:42-47**

[42] Jesus said unto them, If God were your Father, ye would love me: for I proceeded forth and came from God; neither came I of myself, but he sent me.

[43] Why do ye not understand my speech? even because ye cannot hear my word.

[44] Ye are of your father the devil, and the lusts of your father ye will do. He was a murderer from the beginning, and abode not in the truth, because there is no truth in him. When he speaketh a lie, he speaketh of his own: for he is a liar, and the father of it.

[45] And because I tell you the truth, ye believe me not.

⁴⁶ Which of you convinceth me of sin? And if I say the truth, why do ye not believe me?
⁴⁷ He that is of God heareth God's words: ye therefore hear them not, because ye are not of God.

Allow me to comment on some worldly confusion based on the teachings of the LORD:

- Abortions: The word Abortion does not appear in the scriptures. However, we can infer, based on the righteousness of God, that it is not His will that any unborn child be deliberately killed.
    - The Supreme Court has overturned Roe v Wade, which makes abortions illegal throughout the USA unless an individual state has granted it to be legal. With a new governmental administration in place, it is expected that abortions will soon be outlawed in all states within the USA.
    - One side is saying that abortion is against the Christian faith, and the other is saying that the government does not have the right to dictate how a woman uses her body. Unfortunately,

both are wrong. If Jesus is our Lord, then we do not own our bodies.

> *What? know ye not that your body is the temple of the Holy Ghost which is in you, which ye have of God, and ye are not your own?*
> *~ 1 Corinthians 6:19*

Personally, I do not believe in abortion. However, I believe each individual must decide while following the guidance of the Holy Ghost. While I would not knowingly abort a child, I do not have the right to determine such a crucial matter for anyone else! Christians pushing against abortions must recognize that God disapproves of killing in any form unless ordained by the LORD. Reproductive healthcare is a vast concentration that cannot be tackled without the guidance of the Lord.

I was once hospitalized for excruciating abdominal pain that I did not understand. I was rushed into surgery and later told that I had endured an "Ectopic" pregnancy! I had no idea what this was at the time. I discovered that I was pregnant and did not know it, and that the fetus was trying to grow within the right Fallopian tube. As it attempted to grow, the pain would increase until it rendered me helplessly ill! Consequently, after surgery, I was told that I probably would never have children. I never thought of this as having an abortion until the recent discussion surrounding abortions! With this revelation, I cried out to God to forgive me, as this was not an abortion! I didn't even know I was pregnant and would never abort a child! As I wept before the LORD, He assured me that I had NOT elected to abort as the world understands it now, but that my life was being saved! I thank God for His grace and mercy in helping me understand.

I came to understand that anyone genuinely concerned about killing embryos must respond to the many lives needlessly taken with guns! Innocent children are knowingly being slaughtered, and these same individuals who are against abortions for any reason are standing idly by and taking no action. This equates to hypocrisy and is the action of a false Christian, saith the LORD. There is an answer for both sides if they seek the LORD.

- Gay and Lesbian Rights: All people are loved by God, even the Gay community. God expects us to give them the same degree of love if we genuinely love Him, as we have been commanded to love everyone. Shortly after I met, "I AM", I saw the movie Philadelphia. I didn't know what it was about but went with other family members. As soon as I was seated, God began to speak. I was told to listen carefully and understand. God said what I was about to see was never to be personally judged, and I was to treat them with the same respect given to all souls. I was told to leave them alone as worse things were happening in the world. Although I believe that same-sex intercourse does not meet the standards of God, I also know that I am never to judge! This tells me there is more to this subject that has not yet been explained, but it is all in God's hands. It is very hypocritical of church members to judge this segment of society while daily fornicating and living unrighteously and believing that God does not know! He knows ALL.

- Voting Rights/Racial Discrimination: America was founded on principles of racial discrimination, injustice, and slavery. Unfortunately, this is a worldly problem. Satan wants to control all things that belong to God, especially the soul of man. I tell you for certain that no one can truthfully declare their love for the LORD and actively deny others the rights that should be available to all! Our Constitution demands it! God will judge the hearts of all men. What we declare with our mouth has no value unless it is validated in the heart.

I pray that you will search the Scriptures carefully for the "Excepts" of Jesus Christ. These words were also crucial in me experiencing all of God. As I have said previously, the spirit world is water, and Planet Earth consists of 70 percent water! These waters on earth are evil. The human body of mankind is also made of 70% or 3/4th of water. This water within the human body is the human spirit within the body that is either alive and active due to its connection with the Holy Ghost or dead and inactive due to following the enemy of the LORD. Please note that John 3:3, 5 states that except a man is born again, he can't even see God, and that he must be born of water and of the Spirit, or he cannot enter the Kingdom of God! Isn't this the entire point of this book…to enter into the presence of God?

> *Jesus answered and said unto him, Verily, verily, I say unto thee, Except a man be born again, he cannot see the kingdom of God.*
> *~ John 3:3*

> *⁵ Jesus answered, Verily, verily, I say unto thee, Except a man be born of water and of the Spirit, he cannot enter into the kingdom of God.*

> *⁶ That which is born of the flesh is flesh; and that which is born of the Spirit is spirit. ~ John 3:5-6*

How can we enter the Presence of God when Jesus is clearly informing us that unless we are born of "Water and the Spirit," we cannot have or maintain a relationship with the LORD. Wake up and hear what God is saying! Hear and understand the "Change" that He is calling for! If anyone wants to enter God's presence, they must be born again. To be born again is not uniting with a church or declaring that one is saved with the mouth.

~ 28 ~

Born Again…What Does It Mean?

To understand, let's look at what Jesus said regarding this phrase in the scriptures, John 3:5 6 in the preceding chapter. To provide clarity, I will refer to Genesis 6 for further explanation. This scripture shows that God was not pleased with the people of the time. In fact, He declared that His Spirit would no longer dwell with man, as man had become evil through and through!

Genesis 6: 1-7

> *[1] And it came to pass, when men began to multiply on the face of the earth, and daughters were born unto them,*
> *[2] That the sons of God saw the daughters of men that they were fair; and they took them wives of all which they chose.*
> *[3] And the LORD said, My spirit shall not always strive with man, for that he also is flesh: yet his days shall be an hundred and twenty years.*
> *[4] There were giants in the earth in those days; and also after that, when the sons of God came*

in unto the daughters of men, and they bare children to them, the same became mighty men which were of old, men of renown.
⁵ And GOD saw that the wickedness of man was great in the earth, and that every imagination of the thoughts of his heart was only evil continually.
⁶ And it repented the LORD that he had made man on the earth, and it grieved him at his heart. ⁷ And the LORD said, I will destroy man whom I have created from the face of the earth; both man, and beast, and the creeping thing, and the fowls of the air; for it repenteth me that I have made them.

Verse 3 indicates that God removed His Spirit from the body of man and declared him as FLESH! Every imagination of the heart of mankind was completely evil! Before this action, all created souls were endowed with a spirit that was "Holy" at birth. This spirit was and is not designed to remain holy unless it is nourished by the Holy Ghost and/or resting in the presence of the Lord.

Children are born with the ability to love and know God from the moment of their birth. They can hear and see beings within the spiritual realm. Therefore, they have a very keen sense of spiritual discernment. Parents must nourish this spirit within the child to keep it alive! If it is not kept before the Lord, it will soon vanish and be subject to the natural things nearby. Do you get this? The initial spirit granted to the children becomes latent or dead, absent spiritual nourishment! Therefore, the spirit must be born again, as stated by Jesus Christ in the scriptures, or it will never see the kingdom of God. Worse yet, the spirit of all humankind must be born of water AND Spirit, or it cannot even enter the Kingdom of God! This water that I speak of is the "Living Spirit" of God Almighty. Don't forget what Jesus said to the Samaritan woman at the well:

> *Jesus answered and said unto her, If thou knewest the gift of God, and who it is that saith to thee, Give me to drink; thou wouldest have asked of him, and he would have given thee living water. ~ John 4:10*

> *The woman saith unto him, Sir, thou hast nothing to draw with, and the well is deep: from whence then hast thou that living water? ~ John 4:11*

> *He that believeth on me, as the scripture hath said, out of his belly shall flow rivers of living water. ~ John 7:38*

It does not matter how good we remain as we transition from childhood to adulthood. The LORD says that "goodness" is not enough, and we MUST be born again. The only path for this rebirth of the inner spirit is to develop a genuine relationship with the LORD and absolutely surrender the soul and mind unto God! There is no other way. No matter how much we claim to love the Lord with our mouths, God will validate the truth of our words based on the contents of our hearts.

It is a straightforward process of falling in love with God Almighty and allowing the human spirit given to us by God to be intimately joined in a spiritual union with the LORD. There is so much more to say about this subject, but for now, I will not respond further.

~ 29 ~

Reading Resources Approved By God

When I operated TaiVon Fashion Gallery, the custom clothing store that the LORD had me open, one of my customers walked in one day and handed me several boxes of Christian books. Her father had just died and had been head of the Theology Dept at a major university in Michigan. When she started cleaning his office after his death, she was contacted by many professors and friends who wanted books from his library. Yet, most of the books she packed were placed in boxes to be delivered to me! She explained that she knew the books that God wanted me to have. I ended up with an inventory of hundreds of books! The authors I have referenced in this section were all included in this collection. There are a few additional authors whom God has given me over the years that are not listed here, but those approved for this book are the most influential. These books forced me to consider righteousness and Sainthood differently.

Those who are called or believed to be Saints should be

righteous and holy before the LORD God. I have read many books about Sainthood, and they seem to differ in meaning. According to USCCB.org, a Saint is defined as "Saints are **persons in heaven** (officially canonized or not), who lived heroically virtuous lives, offered their life for others, or were martyred for the faith, and who are worthy of imitation." Since none of us can accurately determine who is in heaven or not, or who is truly a hero, the canonized list becomes problematic. Although the Catholic church uses its own rules to canonize determined individuals as "Saints," this does not mean that they are Saints according to the Lord God!

If the standard is that we imitate the actions of those deemed to be "Saints," we must be careful and know what God is saying about the individual. If we allow Him to lead us, he will identify who is righteous or living as He has directed. We are greatly influenced by the opinions of others who might not have sought God for the truth. This especially applies to determining what books to read or which author you should follow. Ask yourself the following questions:

- Does the author believe that Jesus Christ is the Living Son of God and is alive?

- Did you pray about the author you want to follow?

- Did the Lord confirm your request to read the book of your choice?

As God sanctions all that I am allowed to read, the authors outlined in this section have been prominently referenced as choices He set aside for me. Therefore, I declare them to be righteous or have messages for the People of God according to divine revelation.

I encourage you to read all the writings of these authors to better understand who God says is living or have lived righteously before Him. My walk with God was greatly impacted by these Authors, so I do encourage you to read all of them that you can and allow the Lord to guide your path as you go. Amen.

1. **Madame Jeanne Guyon**: Jeanne-Marie Bouvier Guyon is commonly known as Madame Guyon and was born in April 1648 and died in June 1717. She was a devout Catholic who was completely committed to the LORD God Almighty. She was imprisoned from 1695 to 1703 after publishing the book *A Short and Very Easy Method of Prayer*. A friend sent me the book *The Autobiography of Madam Jeanne Guyon* as I was discovering the reality of the LORD.

Through this book, God taught me the power of prayer and the meaning of Resting in His Presence! I also came to realize the power and blessing of being a woman! I encourage all Christian women to read her autobiography immediately. I do warn you that it is not an easy read, but it can be life-changing! I reread this book yearly.

2. **A.W. Tozer**: Tozer is my favorite author! All his teachings are embedded in my soul, and I am convinced that the content is on the scrolls that God gave me to consume at the beginning of my walk with Him. They are all so very familiar. He, too, provides a dire warning to the Church and its leaders as instructed by God.

3. **J. Oswald Sanders**: The first book I read written by Sanders was *"Enjoying Intimacy with God."* The writings in this book compelled me to examine my soul deeply, considering whether I was genuinely enjoying all of God and assessing the fullness of my relationship with Him. As I continued to be ministered to by the Lord and apply the teachings presented by Sanders, my love for God was deepened.

4. **Howard O. Pittman**: Mr. Pittman was the Keynote

Speaker at the first Spiritual Warfare Workshop that I presented to others. God had a local minister bring a copy of the book "Demons: An Eyewitness Account" to my home late one night as I was seeking an understanding of the "things" that were coming into my daily presence. After reading the book, I was instructed by the Lord to call Mr. Pittman and invite him to speak at a workshop. Before the call, I was given the date and location by the Lord. Mr. Pittman initially declined my invitation as he had a previous engagement on the same date. Before I hung up the phone, I advised him that my invitation was at the request of the Lord. I requested that he go back and ask the Lord for advice. He called me back in a few days, saying that God had confirmed to him that he was to accept my invitation.

Mr. Pittman assisted me in presenting 3 Workshops during his lifetime. He was the humblest person I have ever met, and he spoke the same words God was pouring into me. I trusted him so much and considered him a friend. Whether you believe in Demons or not, please read the referenced book and then go to God in prayer.

5. **Brother Lawrence**: I have only read one book written by

Brother Lawrence, but it was profound. It captured my soul and led me in the way of God more than anything that I had learned at the time. As I retained all that I was presented with that had been given by the LORD, I knew what I wanted my life to be. I **purposed** in my heart to KNOW all of Jesus, my Lord. I set my mind on always being in His presence. The more I sought this way of existence, the more love I developed for Him. The deeper our love grew, the less others understood me. Finally, I was able to enter the Presence of my LORD anytime and wherever I pleased! I know this is where God desires me to be. Please read the book, *"The Practice of the Presence of God"* by Brother Lawrence.

6. **O. Hallesby**: This author is best known for his book *"Prayer,"* which is filled with so many powerful reflections of who God is. It too was life-changing for me. I keep this book close and read it at least twice yearly.

7. **Socrates**: This is a man who grew up in Athens as a Greek Philosopher. He believed and worshiped hundreds of gods. Other than Jesus Christ Himself, there is no one that I know that I desire to sit in their presence and quiz their mind than

Socrates! I have not yet found a man, alive or dead, who has so absolutely mimicked the words of God that were spoken to me, as has Socrates! Because he began to live by the words spoken and learned from God, he was tried and sentenced to die. Since he knew God's words to be profoundly truthful, he then agreed to kill himself rather than abandon them. He said he would self-ingest a deadly poison, and he did!

Understand that Socrates was considered a man of much wisdom among men. Therefore, he did not understand why other wise men did not understand his cause. What was he guilty of as a Greek Athenian? Those prosecuting him said, "Socrates is an evil-doer, and a curious person, who searches into things under the earth and in heaven, and he makes the worse appear, the better cause, and he teaches the doctrines described above to others."[10] The real problem was that Socrates had discovered God Almighty, the true God that was unrelated to the hundreds of gods worshipped in Athens! He had forsaken the false gods of Athens and had fallen in love with the LORD God

---

[10] Plato. "Apology of Socrates." *World Literature*, translated by Benjamin Jowett, Indian River State College Libraries, 2018, https://irsc.libguides.com/worldlit/apology.

Almighty! While resting in the presence of the Great, "I AM," he discovered that God knows ALL and that he, as a man, knew nothing, even though he was believed to be filled with wisdom! He recognized that the Wisdom of the LORD God was the most incredible truth on earth and counted himself blessed to be able to claim himself as knowing nothing outside of what he learned from the LORD! Socrates set out to prove that no one was wiser than God Almighty. Therefore, he sought out other men who were considered wise and questioned them about their theories of life or whatever they promoted, to see if they knew anything. He was able to disarm all the men he met, leaving them completely unaware of what they were teaching! He then concluded that he was truly wiser than they, yet he was aware that he knew nothing beyond what God had revealed!

God teaches through stories and questions. Therefore, Socrates had a very unique way of asking questions that caused his opponents to engage in deep self-analysis before answering. This is a technique he received from God Himself! There are those who currently work with personality disorders who claim to use a "Socratic" method of questioning. Such a method is simply manmade and has no value without God!

Quotes from Socrates that can improve our lives and lead us to God: [11]

- "Awareness of ignorance is the beginning of wisdom." ~ Socrates

  - "When the debate is lost, slander becomes the tool of the loser." ~ Socrates

  - "Most people, including ourselves, live in a world of relative ignorance. We are even comfortable with that ignorance because it is all we know. When we first start facing the truth, the process may be frightening, and many people run back to their old lives. But if you continue to seek truth, you will eventually be able to handle it better. In fact, you want more! It's true that many people around you now may think you are weird or even a danger

---

[11] AZQuotes, "Socrates Quotes," accessed March 5, 2025, https://www.azquotes.com/author/37865-Socrates

to society, but you don't care. Once you've tasted the truth, you won't ever want to go back to being ignorant." ~ Socrates

- "True wisdom comes to each of us when we realize how little we understand about life, ourselves, and the world around us." ~ Socrates

- "I know that I am intelligent because I know that I know nothing." ~ Socrates

- "The real danger in life is not death, but living an evil life." ~ Socrates

- "The only true wisdom is in knowing you know nothing." ~ Socrates

8. **Andrew Murray**: The writings of Andrew Murray are additionally profound and will lead the reader to submit to God in a way that is very easy to understand and follow. The books *"Absolute Surrender" and "Humility"* are my favorites.

~ 30 ~

Love is the Answer

Dear Readers, learn to trust the LORD with ALL your heart. This is needed to accomplish the change required by the LORD. Believe that there is nothing greater than experiencing His Precious Love. I promise you that He will quiet every storm and quench every fire that comes your way. The devil cannot stand between you and God unless you allow it to be so! You will be able to walk on hot coals of fire and have no pain when you honestly and truthfully purpose in your heart to have a truly Radical love relationship with the LORD! You can't be stopped…EVER.

There is so much that I have stated in this writing that is confirmed within the Holy Scriptures. The question is, will mankind hear; will YOU listen, hear, and obey the LORD? According to Lord God, there will be a continuation by mankind to follow their own natural mind and the wisdom of evil acts of rebellion against God! LORD have mercy on us all. Amen.

I pray that some portions of my words have encouraged you

to seek the Lord God for added clarity of all that has been written. I ask you to question yourself and determine where you are in Christ Jesus. If you have been faithful to what you believe is the path to worshipping and loving the Lord, yet nothing has changed in your spiritual growth, please consider that there is perhaps more your soul needs to seek. Please do not assume that you "know you are Saved," but go before His Throne and seek His Truths.

Before ending this book, I must inform you of an additional revelation that was not originally intended for this book. Just as I thought I was finished writing, the LORD informed me that this revelation must be included. I will add no comment other than to state what He said:

> *"Many times, I have declared that I will not wait much longer for the inhabitants of the world, and particularly those that claim to be called by my name, to change. Know for sure that time is now very short. Know that there are three things that will bring it all to an end.*

1) False Religion, 2) Rebellion,[12] and 3) Sexual Sin," Thus saith the LORD.

"The strongman is here. He is committed to saturating the mind of all with his evil ways and thoughts. He does know that his time also is at an end. Open your hearts to Me, the LORD of all, that you are no longer deceived. Hear my voice as My sheep know my voice, saith the LORD God. Draw nigh to me and I will restore you once again to Me."

I have said what God has asked me to say. Although I want to present so much more I will not. There are many other mysteries that impact our daily lives! Before presenting more, the LORD wants to see if we truly want to walk in His truths. Perhaps additional mysteries will be revealed at the request of the LORD later. Only God knows! However, the best direct reminder that I can provide is captured in the scriptures below as recorded in Revelation 3:15-22.

---

[12] Rebellion here refers to the rejection of the LORD and His teachings. The walking away from His righteousness and embracing evil on all levels.

Revelation 3:15-22

¹⁵ I know thy works, that thou art neither cold nor hot: I would thou wert cold or hot.

¹⁶ So then because thou art lukewarm, and neither cold nor hot, I will spue thee out of my mouth.

¹⁷ Because thou sayest, I am rich, and increased with goods, and have need of nothing; and knowest not that thou art wretched, and miserable, and poor, and blind, and naked:

¹⁸ I counsel thee to buy of me gold tried in the fire, that thou mayest be rich; and white raiment, that thou mayest be clothed, and that the shame of thy nakedness do not appear; and anoint thine eyes with eyesalve, that thou mayest see.

¹⁹ As many as I love, I rebuke and chasten: be zealous, therefore and repent.

²⁰ Behold, I stand at the door, and knock: if any man hear my voice, and open the door, I will come in to him, and will sup with him, and he with me.

²¹ To him that overcometh will I grant to sit with me in my throne, even as I also overcame, and am set down with my Father in his throne.

²² He that hath an ear, let him hear what the Spirit saith unto the churches.

And I saw a new heaven and a new earth: for the first heaven and the first earth were passed away; and there was no more sea. ~ Revelation 21:1

May we all pray for true revival and change as charged by God! May we all strive to Rest in the Presence of the LORD as we allow Him to guide us daily in all aspects of our lives.

Be blessed in all matters as you humbly seek God Almighty. I promise you that He will welcome you into His Presence if you are sincere in your desire to Know Him! I remain always available to those who want to know more about my personal interactions with the Great I AM THAT I AM. Amen.

Always in Christ Jesus
Zelma McKinney
Minister of God's WORD

May the LORD God Truly Bless
You as You go Forward

Section V

Student Testimonies

Each year, I evaluate my students based on their retained knowledge of the teachings and revelations brought to us by God. They submit annual written reports that explain their level of understanding and gains. I have included a few here that could shed further light on the contents of this writing and their ability to hear what the LORD is saying. I obtained permission to include a few of them in this book. No names are provided to protect individual privacy.

Student Testimony #1

I met Minister McKinney for the first time in 2004 when she and her husband came to visit Los Angeles, CA. Her daughter was engaged to my oldest son, and they were preparing to get married soon.

Then again, 12 years later, in May 2016, my son and her husband came to Los Angeles, CA, and picked me up as I was in dire straits. I was a drug user, drinking alcohol, sexually promiscuous, practicing idolatry, African Voodoo, living in filth, and, unknown to me at the time, possessed by demons. Instead, the truth be told, the devil himself possessed me, and he had taken control of my life.

So, my son brought me to Riverside, CA, where he, his wife, Minister McKinney, and her husband lived at the time. But, before I moved into their home, I was taken to a mental care facility where I had to detox from all the drugs and alcohol usage.

Be put on medications as I was diagnosed as having schizophrenia and being bipolar. I was also suffering from depression as my late husband had passed away in 1995 just before the birth of my youngest child, a daughter, whom my son had the sense and understanding/wisdom from Minister McKinney and God to take custody away from me with the lifestyle that I was living. She came to live with the McKinney's when she was in middle school, growing up in a Christian household.

It was in May 2016 when I was fortunate enough to be able to move into her home. She immediately began praying for me, praying with me, anointing me, and casting out the demons possessing me. I was given many books to read, study, and complete assignments on. She gave me my first Holy Bible, and I became a DMSM student and a member of the I AM Loves Me group, in October 2017, attending the Boot Camp.

I wasn't a Christian before I met her. Sure, I attended church occasionally and prayed sometimes. But I was a sinner living in worldly ways and doing all sorts of evil. I had not been saved by God.

My life has totally and completely changed since I've been with Minister McKinney and DMSM in so many ways. I prayed constantly, "Lord, Change Me. Change Me, Lord," and He did. I prayed, "Lord God, dissect my soul," and He did. When I think back to when I first moved in with the McKinney's, I can remember how the devil had taken control of my life. I was still taking the medications for treating mental illness. I was saying that I could speak over 500 different languages. I was being tempted and led by the devil and demons in big and small ways, not knowing and understanding about being a true Christian.

Minister McKinney, DMSM, and the LORD God Almighty saved me from total destruction. By prayer, petitioning, and submission to Jesus Christ as my personal Savior, I confessed and repented of my sins, asked for forgiveness, and continued to denounce the devil from having any control of my life.

I am so grateful and thankful for the love of God and how He protected me. I am a living testimony of how God can change your life. If it had not been for Minister McKinney, Dissect My Soul Ministries, and my family, I probably would have been dead by now, and that's the truth.

I believe in all of the revelations taught within this ministry because I am able to witness and experience some of them firsthand, which is truly a blessing. I see how God is moving and what He has done in Minister McKinney's life, her family, myself, my family, and the DMSM group, as well as others that are around us.

There is only One True and Living God, and I'm praying and planning on being ready when He comes. My desire is to fall completely in Love with Jesus Christ! Not just saying the words but giving my whole life to Him. I'm praying, tarrying, and surrendering my whole heart to God. I'm seeking and pursuing God each and every day, staying focused on Jesus and looking to Him alone to supply all of my needs.

I am removing the lies and replacing them with the truth - which is the Word of God. I'm looking to God's word when being attacked by the tempter, which leads to me following God with obedience and freedom, renewing my mind, body, and spirit, and focusing on Jesus Christ. I'm claiming the victory in the Name of Jesus and following God's plan and not my own by doing His will because He is in complete control of everything.

My daily prayer is this: Jesus, I want to fall more in Love with you. Help me to do it from a Heart that wishes and desires to know you better rather than just for what you can do for me. Help me, Lord Jesus, to cultivate spiritual awareness to know what is coming from you, your word, the Truth, and what is coming from the devil, temptations, lies, and deceit.

Lord Jesus, I choose you, and I need your help fighting and winning this battle daily against Satan and the evil that is all around. Thank you, Lord, for being my Savior and for Loving me. Thank you for a family that Loves me and helps me to Love you more each day, knowing and understanding the ultimate sacrifice that you made for us.

I LOVE YOU, JESUS,

Amen

Scripture to live by

Deuteronomy 6:4-7

The LORD our God is one LORD: and thou shalt love the LORD thy God with all thine heart, and with all thy soul, and with all thy might. And these words, which I command thee this day, shall be in thine heart: and thou shalt teach them diligently unto thy children, and shalt talk of them when thou sittest in thine house, and when thou walkest by the way, and when thou liest down, and when thou risest up.

I'm still living with Minister McKinney and continue studying and learning so much from her about developing a personal relationship with Almighty God.

Student Testimony #2

I met Minister McKinney in 1988 when my ex-husband made a business deal with her, and consequently, she invited me to an overnight prayer workshop in her clothing store. My life has never been the same as this propelled my faith-filled journey with Christ.

I was not a Christian when we met. My parents and aunt raised me as a Catholic. I had 12 years of Catholic education which gave me some kind of reverence towards God though filled with too many rituals and erroneous idol worshipping.

Through her teachings, I came to trust in God my Father, Jesus Christ my Lord and Savior, and our precious Holy Ghost, our forever Comforter! Only by God's grace and mercy did I survive and cope with my mentally abusive marriage. Consequently, I waited until both of my children were adults to stand on the biblical term of being "unequally yoked" and got divorced. Through her teachings, I came to trust and know Jesus more profoundly. Since then, I have remarried and have two beautiful grandchildren.

I can honestly say I have no idea where I would be now if it were not for DMSM! Minister McKinney's Biblically based teachings in this ministry are brought forth just as God instructs her to speak and teach. Nothing more and nothing less as she is an anointed vessel and anointed minister of our Lord Jesus Christ. DMSM has redirected my spiritual understanding of what it means to be the type of Christian our Lord and Savior wants us to be, which is not what I was before. I humbly now know that when some storms come my way, I hold fast to my favorite verse: "Be still and know that I am God!"

It has been such a rewarding and true blessing for my family and me to be a part of this ministry. God has protected my family and me from so much. I will forever be grateful to God for allowing us to be a part of DMSM and for Minister McKinney's everlasting love and obedience to God. She has not only taught us God's truths but also has loved, prayed, guided, inspired, and strengthened my family and me and many others.

I believe the revelations that are taught by Minister McKinney! As an anointed Minister of Jesus Christ, she explains her encounters, experiences, and total truths of what God has revealed to her in a way that if we have ears to hear, the revelations flood our souls with love and awe for God! I have listened to other ministers, preachers, and pastors, and not one of them teaches the way she does. She teaches from her inner being, where God has stored up all that she teaches and will say in the future as well! Only if you are anointed and chosen to speak what "Thus says the Lord" can you penetrate man's hearts the way Minister McKinney does!

She has always told us to "take it back to the Lord" if we doubt, and He will confirm it for us, and He always does!

I have studied with Minister McKinney for over 30 years. I give God the honor, glory, and praise that I have been privileged to hear His Truths with His anointed Minister. I really look forward to our weekly classes.

It is not enough for me to know that Jesus Christ is the only way to salvation, and I have accepted Him into my heart with all the pretty cliché Christian words of being born again, etc. I am seeking to enter into His presence in order to abide and commune with Him as I seek His face continuously. Seek ye first the Kingdom of God comes to my mind daily. I ask God to Dissect My Soul many times daily, every day, and to crucify my flesh. As I grow in Christ, I am also asking God to meet me "at the top of the mountain" through a richer and deeper prayer life that He is currently teaching me. Total surrender is essential as our will can't exist in order that He may direct our path and lives as His will is done! Obedience to Him and only Him daily is necessary as we put God first and foremost, even if this means everyone else comes second or third. Love God with all of your heart, mind, and soul. I know the promises He has graciously given me, and I stand firm, trusting only Jesus! The enemy does his job, which is to steal, kill, and destroy. I will overcome his tactics as long as I submit immediately (prayer) to Christ. Absolute surrender and obedience to Him daily is my heart's desire, and having humility intertwined with helplessness. I have been a member of DMSM for many years, and it has been an enormous blessing, and I look forward to whatever God has in store for us as a ministry. Meanwhile, as an older member, I pray that I can inspire and share my personal experiences with the younger generation when they reach out. I will always ask God to lead me with this, "may the words of my mouth and the meditation of my heart be acceptable unto you, Oh Lord!" Amen!

Student Testimony #3

I was raised by a Christian Mother and was fortunate to have met Minister McKinney when I was a child. My Dad came into Minister McKinney's life and then told my Mom about Minister McKinney, and they both became friends. This is a true blessing for me, and I often thank God for it. Minister McKinney counseled me a few times when I was young as I was troubled by demonic spirits in my home and did not understand what was happening. The LORD showed Minister McKinney what was going on in my life. She helped me to trust in the blood that Jesus had shed for me.

In my early 20's, I participated in Minister McKinney's ministry by attending her seminars. Once I was older, I became a student of her awesome On-Line Bible Classes and quickly became a devoted, loyal member of Dissect My Soul Ministries.

My Christian walk has changed since I started studying with

Dissect My Soul Ministries, as it helped me during a very difficult time in my life when my parents got divorced. I always leaned on His Everlasting Love to get me through it all. Minister McKinney has taught me to crucify my flesh and submit/surrender myself to Jesus. This has Blessed me in many ways! Through the teachings of DMSM and the constant encouragement from Minister McKinney, I am no longer the shy young man I was before. I have found all the confidence that I need in Christ Jesus. Even though I have gone through some challenges, I always remember my favorite Bible Verse that teaches me that I Can do all things through Christ who strengthens me!

I believe in the revelations taught within this Ministry. Through prayer, God has comforted my heart in knowing the revelations Minister McKinney teaches are from The Great I AM. These truths have opened my eyes, given me clarity, renewed strength, and continued hope. I am so thankful and very appreciative that God has given me so many revelations through the teachings from Dissect My Soul Ministries.

I confidently walk in humbleness and humility as I strive for perfection in the Lord. I would try to be an example to others as I share this path that I have chosen. From my experiences, I know God sees all and protects us when we need to be protected. I thank God that He sent Minister McKinney my way. I say to all parents…love and protect your children as Satan is waiting and watching to harm them behind closed doors! It is only by God's grace and mercy that you can guide and protect them. This journey is a continued one, and with all that I have been taught, it gives me greater confidence to seek the more of who God is. I pray I can obediently follow God for the rest of my life while loving Him with my whole heart! I look forward to gaining and receiving more understanding of all God has for me in my life according to His Perfect Will.

Student Testimony #4

My wife had known Minister McKinney for several years. When we went to Minister McKinney's daughter's wedding in California, I met Minister McKinney for the first time in 2007.

I have studied with Minister McKinney for 15+ years. Before I met her, I believed in God, went to church, and tried to live a "good life." However, I was not a Christian because I did not have a relationship with Jesus.

Minister McKinney has shaped me by teaching the Truth God Himself has revealed. I am grateful God has changed me from the inside out! Once I learned in my heart that Jesus Loves me and wants us to Love Him by living in a relationship with Him, then I began pursuing Him, and the layers of the onion were peeled back (my hardened heart) - as I totally repented and chose Jesus as my Lord and Savior. I absolutely surrendered self. As we studied in Revelations 3:20, I heard His knock on my heart, opened the door, and let Jesus in. I became Born again!

The revelations she taught us are all Biblical and available for those with ears to hear and eyes to see. For example, Matthew 13 correlates with the revelation that 3/4ths of Christians are on their way to Hell and do not even know it. Another lesson about prayer taught to us is that it should come from a state of helplessness and faith. Lastly, our study of Proverbs was profound as we learned how Precious, Powerful, and Special to God that Wisdom is.

I am applying what I learned from Proverbs by trusting God and leaning on His understanding, not my own. I am praying, "God, make me holy and selfless." Asking God to fill my mind with thoughts from Him as I reject any thoughts from the enemy. I am keeping my eyes fixed on Jesus and abiding while loving God with all of my heart, mind, soul, and strength, as well as loving others. I am resisting and fleeing Satan, relying on God to fight my battles for me, as only He can win them. Resting in His arms/presence - letting go while enjoying God's comfort, peace, and grace.

Student Testimony #5

God brought Minister McKinney into my life in an unexpected way. I had been married for less than two years to someone I didn't know very well. We were very different people from different backgrounds: cultural, socio-economic, educational, etc. We were miserable, but I believed in being married for life. I wasn't a Christian. Though Jesus wasn't part of my daily life, I still knew I would be faithful and stay married once I said "I Do" before God. I struggled with navigating my role in the marriage.

I attended a Woman's Day Program at a local church. Minister McKinney was preaching at the event. She spoke on the order of the family. As I sat and listened, I realized God was answering the turmoil I had in my heart about my marriage. My family wasn't aligned in God's order. He was the answer to my problems and my marriage. After the service, I introduced myself to her and let her know what her words meant to me. We have been together since. I've studied with her for over 27 years now. She has helped my family in so many ways over the years. God has continued to show me my past isn't something that makes Him reject me. He knew me before the foundation of the world. He loves me so much. He sent Jesus to bring me back to Him.

I believe all the revelations God used her to share with us. The scriptures support every one of them. I remember one day in the summer of 2017. I received a phone call from Minister McKinney. She told me she had just seen Jesus at a Wendy's restaurant! My heart rejoiced with her. I've watched God use her to bring the Bible to life for me countless times. This was another example of how He is the same yesterday, today, and forever. One of the beautiful things about God is that He NEVER changes! If we read about things He said or did in scripture, they still apply to us today. Therefore, we can find hope in Him. Hope in His Truths. Hope and peace, knowing we can trust Him. Amen!

www.ingramcontent.com/pod-product-compliance
Lightning Source LLC
Chambersburg PA
CBHW070049080526
44586CB00013B/983